How We Preach: Preaching in the African Context

by

Bishop Eben Kanukayi Nhiwatiwa

Africa Ministry Series

How We Preach: Preaching in the African Context

Cover and interior design: Karin Wizer
Cover photo: © Murali Nath | Dreamstime.com
Typesetting: PerfecType, Nashville, TN

ISBN 978-0-88177-866-3

Contents

Preface

This book is one of two volumes on *Preaching in the African Context*. In volume one, I explore *Why We Preach* and the *principles* of contextual preaching in Africa. In this second volume, I explore *How We Preach* and the *practice* of contextual preaching in Africa. The two volumes go hand in hand; the principles need good practice to become contextual preaching, and our practice needs principles to ensure integrity. The two volumes together are intended to address the dearth of literature on preaching from an African point of view that I saw while on the Faculty of Theology at Africa University.

There is compelling need in theological education to teach and study all disciplines contextually. I sensed the need for a preaching text that pulls together information from existing literature and texts for the African preacher. Discussions with students from all corners of Africa helped me contextualize preaching. It is presumptuous to write a book on preaching that does justice to the divergent experiences in Africa. But shared experiences can be adapted and applied to particular contexts.

Contextual preaching serves as the most appropriate way of communicating the gospel in Africa: it can connect with people and engage the minds of the people in effective ways. It is incumbent upon African theologians to preach the gospel in ways that recognize African cultural modes of communication. African preachers are not oblivious to the need for cultural sensitivity. The use of vernacular languages in African churches is in itself a milestone in the process of contextualization

Congregational responses with ululating or song accompanied by drums, rattles, and dancing are positive signs of a people worshipping in context. What preachers still lack is intentionality towards contextual preaching. This observation is further affirmed Episcopal Area. My aim in this book is to provide pastors and lay preachers with the practices that will help them be more sensitive to African cultural nuances.

Finally this book is for both seasoned preachers and beginners, including students in seminaries, Bible colleges, and universities. Preaching is an urgent aspect of ministry that can open new horizons and give fresh outlook for the future. Christian preaching is sustained by the belief in the resurrection of Jesus Christ.

Acknowledgments

First and foremost, I wish to thank Africa University for according me sabbatical leave for study. Further, a special word of appreciation goes to Professors Edward P. Wimberly and Anne Streaty Wimberly for facilitating my family's one-month stay at the Interdenominational Theological Center, Atlanta, Georgia, USA, and for arranging for me to use the Clark Atlanta University Library. To all preachers whose sermons found their way in this study I say thank you. In addition, a word of thanks goes to Mrs. Redempter Gambinga, the typist who fed my longhand manuscript into the computer at the Ocasia Typing Services in Mutare, for her patience and diligence. More expression of thanks go to Mrs. Patience Gwaradzimba, my secretary in the Bishop's office, for sorting out material of the book for rewriting as required by the editor.

My wife, Greater Tarememredzwa, and daughter Nyasha left me undisturbed for long hours while I worked on the book. I thank them for their patience and encouragement. To all present and former students in my Homiletics class, I am grateful for the discussions and divergent views we shared whose fruits have found their way into this book. In addition, I thank and dedicate this book to my first professor of Homiletics, the late Reverend Dr. Maurice Culver, and to my late pastor at Old Mutare Mission, the Reverend David Mudzengerere, who encouraged me to join the ordained ministry. Reverend Mudzengerere urged me: "Nhiwatiwa, kana uchiparidza usazotamba nevanhu," translated literally, "Nhiwatiwa, when you preach don't ever play with people."

Finally, allow me to thank a team of co-workers who later became involved in this book as if by divine providence. Reverend Steve Bryant and Mrs. Kara Lassen Central Conferences in Africa to produce devotional and theological education material for the church and seminaries. It was during such processes and discussion that Steve got to know of my manuscript and became interested. With instant insight, Kara suggested that the manuscript could be divided into two books: the first part focusing on the theory of preaching and the second on the practical side of it. Without their support this work would still be in the shape of a manuscript. To the General Board of Discipleship I say thank you for seeing something of substance in these books as worth publishing under your auspices.

Finally, to Kathleen Stephens, my editor for the books, for putting a refining touch to the manuscript and thereby shaping the material into readable books, I say thank you. It is indeed my hope to always take preaching seriously, as Reverend Mudzengerere urged me. May this book inspire more preachers in their proclamation of the gospel.

E. K. N.

Chapter 1

Preparing to Preach

Before taking off, airplane flight crews explain to passengers the measures to take in case of emergency. These potential emergencies are usually major, such as lack of pressure in the cabin, which means there will be no oxygen on emergency landing. There is no mention of crashing, although that is what is implied. In one aircraft the captain advised us to listen to the instructions "in the unlikely event there could be a problem." The point is that despite technological advancements, careful inspections by qualified technicians, and detailed preparations before a flight, one cannot rule out the possibility of a disaster.

Similarly, preparing to preach is no guarantee that the sermon will not crash-land. The difference in the analogy is that airplane passengers are instructed on what precautions to take. But no one informs the poor congregation of what to watch for in a sermon so that they can leave the sanctuary for their own safety! We however urge preachers to take stages in the preparation of sermons seriously, if for no other reason than that those disasters might be mitigated, and above all to be most ready for the upliftment of the Spirit in communicating God's message to the people with power.

The Situation of the African Preacher

In modern business language there is talk about conditions of service, a term meaning rules, codes of conduct, and benefits due to the employee. What is usually not considered in the conditions of service is the general environment in which the individual employee will find him or herself. The larger environment impacts the performance and productivity of the employee beyond that of the immediate location. The environment within which the African preacher operates should be examined with the aim of determining some constraining factors that might negatively affect delivery of sermons.

Preaching demands thorough preparation involving the whole being of the preacher. It is hard, time-consuming work to minister at one's best. There are, however, factors that hinder the African preacher from paying attention to the preparation of sermons. Habit and tradition play a part in this. Africans are generally impromptu speakers. This self-assured confidence can lead to preaching without preparation. Impromptu speaking is an ability and skill that can enhance one's oral delivery, but when it leads to little preparation it hinders the ability to preach well.

Another factor is that African preachers are generally overworked and exhausted most of the time. Consequently, they are usually deprived of adequate time to prepare for sermons. One may hear a pastor at a church function on a Saturday stating with surprise that tomorrow is Sunday and that he or she is the one preaching. This usually indicates that the pastor has not finished preparing the next day's sermon or, worse, has not begun preparation.

Pastoral visitation is the norm in the African church, yet the majority of African pastors have no private means of transport. This is particularly hard on those in rural areas. Parishioners must be visited, so the pastor does so by walking from one house to another throughout the village. If a member is not home, that pastor may have to walk to the fields to find him or her, which could be five or more kilometres away. On returning home from visiting members, the pastor may hear that a member has died at a neighbouring village where another preaching point is situated. To be a good pastor means that one must not rest but proceed to be with the bereaved family.

In a village setting and at mission centres the pastor often plays the role of kraal head. Travellers, who usually arrive late in the evening, need to be fed and housed, no matter how late it is. All this must be done despite the pastor's weariness from the day of walking. Urban pastors may be relatively better off, but there are a number of circumstances that also crowd their workday and leave little time for preparing a sermon.

A further complication is the lack of education and resources. Homiletic tools for crafting sermons that are readily available in the Western world are in most cases nonexistent for the African preacher. Pastors often graduate from seminaries with only the textbook prescribed for each of the courses they took. Indeed, many student pastors depend on the library because books are so expensive if they are available at all. This means that even a well-trained preacher may dry up intellectually because of lack of resources. Compounding the problem is the fact that most African churches are being served by preachers who do not have much formal education.[1]

To survive in the pulpit, preachers may fall into the temptation of preaching superficial sermons. Those blessed with musical talent may use three quarters of the sermon time for singing and one quarter for narrative. In some cases the pastor repeats the same sermon with minimal changes. Or, pastors may preach another's sermon as if it were their own. Speaking of preachers who face similar challenges in Korea, Chang Bok Chung said, "Plagiarism of sermon material is a serious problem among the many preachers. Since Korean pastors are pressed by their heavy schedule, they prefer to copy other people's sermons without putting in their own effort. Therefore, the creativity and freshness of the message in the pulpit is not experienced as much."[2] Based on some sermons I have heard in Zimbabwe, one could say the same, that they lack the depth of content and evidence of serious preparation to engage both the mind and heart of the listener.

I present this in the hope that the African preacher will approach the task of preaching fully aware of the hurdles. A problem whose dimensions are clearly understood is a problem halfway solved. African people face numerous problems emanating from lack of resources and other prevailing conditions, but they usually overcome them by their resourcefulness. In discussing the intricacies of preparing to preach with all the implied capacities of the preacher, my hope is that the pastor will be encouraged to dig into her or his kit of resourcefulness to fill the gaps.

General Views on Preparing to Preach

A cross-section of ideas on what is involved in preparing to preach readily exists. There is a general agreement among homileticians that study is an important element in the preparation of sermons.[3] This could be studying the particular text, the Bible as a whole, or other books. As we have already noted, study as practiced in the West regarding preparation for preaching is the weakest link for the African preacher. But where study is carefully considered during the preparation of a sermon, greater is the reward.

The preacher's awareness of the congregation is another crucial element in preparing a sermon. Samuel Proctor calls this contextual awareness of the congregation "the ecology of the sermon."[4] Knowing the congregation is not an easy task, especially for the African people. While Africans talk so much about communal life, they can be very closed in their private lives. It takes time for the African to trust and open up to another. The pastor often is viewed as a stranger who should be kept at the periphery of a member's or family's concerns. Young pastors have to work harder than others to gain the trust of members, since age is usually equated with wisdom in matters of life experience. In some cases, cultural traditions can keep Africans from truly knowing one another. For example, the Manyika, an ethnic group found mainly in the Northeastern part of Zimbabwe, traditionally respond positively in conversation with others, even when the truth is the opposite. Such customs can be a barrier for a preacher who is attempting to know the people. Being aware that it is hard to know what makes your people tick is an important element of knowing them.

In most cases, it is possible to get to know one's congregation. By visiting them, a pastor gains information on age groups, career patterns, social stratification, general community interests, and networks of relationships in the congregation. African congregations have a web of relationships interwoven by totems, extended families, and marital connections. A misunderstanding with one person may affect the preacher's relationships with a large section of the congregation because of the relational connections. Knowing the congregation also means the literal sense of visualizing the faces of individual members seated in the sanctuary listening to your sermon. As you prepare the sermon with these faces in mind, the sermon becomes personalized for the individuals in question. This is why guest preachers should be used only occasionally rather than on a regular basis.

One more concept regarding the preparation of a sermon is that the process involves the molding of the person behind the preaching. In *Preaching the Story*, Charles Rice writes, "I have learned in the whole process of sermon preparation from choosing a text or topic to hearing what that particular text says to my particular pastoral situation, to finding a form that fits content and preacher and congregation—I am ultimately preparing a person rather than a product."[5] Rice continues, "The embodied word calls for the preparation of one's whole being, including the body, for this holy vocation." He goes on to say, "Whatever form it takes, without careful, intentional discipline no artist succeeds, and it is as true of the preacher as of the actor or dancer that we must put our whole being, including our bodies into the task."[6]

I am reminded of a schoolmate of mine who was a superstar in soccer. He expressed enthusiasm for the sport by telling us that in the game he was going to leave his leg in the soccer pitch. Such an expression indicated how he put his whole self into the game. Similarly, keep this verse in mind as you prepare and preach your sermon: "Therefore, since we are surrounded by so great a cloud of witnesses, let us also lay aside every weight, . . . and let us run with perseverance the race that is set before us" (Heb. 12:1). So, being cheered by these witnesses, the preacher puts everything into the sermon with the hope that he/she will not fail them. In my African belief system that the dead are living and participate with us in life, though in mysterious ways, I envision people of faith known to me who are resting in the Lord as concrete representatives of this cloud of witnesses watching my performance in proclaiming the Word. Each preacher discovers his or her own way of evoking a transcendent feeling in preparing and delivering sermons.

Crucial Steps in Preparing To Preach

We have discussed some different aspects and general views concerning the preparation of preaching. There are some specific stages that every preacher follows in one way or the other. The preacher should not be surprised to have an insight that best suits the conclusion of a sermon and yet have no sense at the time which sermon idea could be developed to match that ending. This is to say there are no rigid rules in preaching but tested principles that have yielded positive results throughout the ages. We will now look at some of the steps the preacher goes through in preparing a sermon. The list is not exhaustive. Through experience and wide reading the preacher will be able to add to the list.

Prayer

Homileticians feel obliged to remind preachers to begin the process of preparing sermons with prayer.[7] One would hope that every preacher realizes the importance of prayer without being reminded. There is a difference in knowing that one must pray and then not do it, and not knowing that one must pray. I am inclined to think that most preachers who neglect prayer are fully aware of their need for prayer. Perhaps we separate Jesus Christ, the message to be preached, from Jesus Christ, the practitioner who should be our model in preaching. Scripture indicates that Jesus Christ usually began an important event or activity with prayer. His ministry began with an extended period of focusing on God through fasting (Matt. 4:2). In choosing his disciples Jesus Christ went out to the mountain to pray and continued praying to God the whole night (Luke 6:12). We all know of the vigil in the Garden of Gethsemane as Jesus Christ prepared to face the Cross. Following in the Lord's footsteps, the preacher must be a person of prayer at all times, including when preparing for preaching.

The preacher's prayer is a humble admission to God that the task belongs to the Creator. Through this kind of prayer the preacher both listens to and talks to God. We ask God that the fullness of his Word be revealed to us. In prayer we let God know our fears, doubts, weaknesses, and strengths, and ask God to mold us into something acceptable and whole for the congregation.

Further, prayer is a source of inspiration in spiritual matters for all those who believe. As one preacher put it, "Preparation may bring a preacher to the pulpit, but prayer will bring the Holy Spirit there."[8] In the African traditional religion, prayer preceded most family and community events. Hunting episodes, planting and harvesting, and community festivals are first presented to God through prayer.[9] The African preacher also can rely on prayers like these when preparing to preach.

The Sermon Idea

Even though there is an endless list of sermon topics and themes available, preachers still struggle with what to preach. It is a misconception to think that the problem is less burdensome when using the lectionary as a source. The truth is that having a text already selected is no guarantee that the preacher will have something to say. Irrespective of the difficulties, clearly identifying the sermon idea is all-important in sermon development. Without a clear understanding of what is to be preached, there is no sermon. Sometimes among homileticians there is too much concern about methods of communication at the expense of the message itself. Polished methods in communicating the gospel with a flimsy message will amount to nothing but a fabulous display of gimmicks.

Where then does the preacher get ideas for preaching? The Bible is the first and foremost source for sermon planning. The Bible contains the great inexhaustible sermon whose theme is God's plan for salvation. From this source, preachers draw and develop ideas to meet the specific needs of their congregations. Since every human situation is mirrored in the Bible, it is the ultimate source for preachers. There is some misunderstanding that getting an idea from the lectionary is different from getting themes from the Bible. The lectionary is based on the Bible and helps both the preacher and the congregation to focus on selected major themes in the Christian faith.

Another way to find sermon ideas is to start with the glaring issues in the congregation, immediate community, or nation as a whole. Choosing sermon themes apart from the lectionary has its own strengths and weaknesses. In this approach the responsibility for deciding what the congregation needs to hear rests heavily on the preacher. The preacher may tend to select his or her favorite themes or those of past sermons that were successful. This is more likely to happen when preachers lack time to adequately prepare.

Simply put, ideas for development of sermons come from everyday life.[10] To be alert to such possibilities, the preacher may keep a notebook to record some happenings for future use as sermon material. What makes a sermon good is not that the idea has never been heard before. It is instead the preacher's ability to develop and communicate ordinary ideas in an extraordinary way. South African president Thabo Mbeki has said that the twenty-first century is the century for the African Renaissance. This statement is memorable not because the words are new, but because the pattern in which those words appear together create a powerful thought regarding development for the African continent. As Phillips Brooks put it, "The best sermon of any time is that times' best utterance . . . So I think that a man's best sermon is the best utterance of his life."[11] Study, observations, conversations in the marketplace, news bulletins, germs of ideas from other preachers—all are vital sources for sermon ideas. As Edgar N. Jackson said, "Sermons do not happen. They grow. They root in life, branch in experience, and blossom in that creative interplay of minds that is the ideal preacher-listener relationship."[12]

In the African traditional religion of the Shona culture, people had the privilege of initiating what they would like to hear from the oracle. Representatives of the people went to the Mwari cult in Matopos to consult with the oracle on issues they felt were important.[13] Similarly, hearers of the gospel need to be able to consult with the preacher in their search for the voice of God on certain issues. On occasion, church members have inquired about what I thought on a particular issue. One time, some money-making clubs mushroomed in Zimbabwe, leading to police investigations of claims that people were being swindled out of their hard-earned cash. Some Christians were ambivalent about the issue and needed biblical and theological guidance based on faith in God. When preachers are mute on such issues people may yearn to consult an oracle. Even if the issue does not concern the majority of worshippers, that particular message can bring back the one sheep to rejoin the ninety-nine in the fold.

Concerted focus on an idea for the sermon does not necessarily mean that is what the congregation will hear. It is common for preachers to hear positive comments about aspects of a sermon that they did not imagine to be the salient features for the listener. In Zimbabwe most denominations organize communities into sections where people meet in small family groups. After the preaching at a section, people are usually given time to respond to the sermon. This is a rare opportunity for the preacher to get feedback from the listeners. I usually am amazed by the multifaceted ways a sermon gets to the ears of the listener. I have stopped telling people what the focus of the sermon is in order to let their minds wander as freely as possible.

The notion that a text has only one point needs some review. Commentaries accentuate this one point in a biblical text. A preacher who approaches the text determined to pinpoint that one point will "shut down all other possible interpretations for their listeners by insistence that their meaning is only one," as Paul Scott Wilson said.[14] We preachers need an idea to organize our thoughts, but at the same time we must be flexible enough to let people hear the word they are attuned to. Ultimately though the word that is received by the hearer is not determined by the preacher alone. As one preacher said, "A sermon has many ears but only one mouth."[15]

Exegesis of the Text for Preaching

Exegesis is the process by which the contemporary reader understands the biblical text in the context of its biblical world. The effort is based on the fact that the Bible is not one book but books that were written by different authors for different readers at different times. The language used reflects the socioeconomic, political, and the historical world of that time.

After getting an idea for a sermon, we assume the preacher will then select the text, since sermon ideas should come from a biblical text. In selecting the text the preacher should determine the beginning and ending of the pericope that retains the gist of the story, event, or episode in a meaningful way. Using segments of the text in a way that distorts the story hinders the listener from hearing the Word from the Bible.

Another assumption we make is that before exegesis, preachers already have put together a great deal of material based on their insights and background material on the topic. Then, commentaries and other books used in the process of exegesis can discourage the preacher from whatever ideas he or she has been entertaining. The African pastor relies heavily on his or her imagination in creating a sermon from the biblical text, and so should exegete the text for an informed point of view.

In his analysis of sermons preached by Chewa preachers of Malawi, Ernst R. Wendland observed that there was no comprehensive exegesis of the texts. He said: "Thus, the crucial issue of widespread ignorance about the Scriptures and what they have to say in their own contextual setting (historical, sociocultural, geographical, etc.) is not being adequately addressed."[16] This view of African preachers as oblivious to the historical context of the text is vividly explained by Horst Burkle. Burkle says that for the African the past is existentially lived and experienced in the present. There is "no real gap separating the past from the present."[17] The African theologian and philosopher John S. Mbiti affirms that the African's sense of time merges the past with the present. "But for both the community and the individual, the most vivid moment is the NOW point . . . " said Mbiti.[18]

Nevertheless, it is inadequate to say that African preachers do not search the historical circumstances of a text only because they have no sense of history. African preachers bridge the gap separating the text in history and the present by using their imaginations. Many of them do not have the necessary skills and tools needed for a thorough job of exegeting the text.

Evangelist Shadrack Wame, whose sermons Wendland studied, did not receive formal training in preaching. God chose him when he was a gardener and formed a preacher out of him.[19] We would not say that Wame did not exegete the text merely because he lacked a sense of history. It is lack of training instead that deprives such African preachers of a clear appreciation of the need for exegetical preparation as an essential element in preaching. Further, we should also remember that textual exegesis is not confined to historical criticism. Exegesis is a homiletical mine shaft that leads to invaluable information for the benefit of the hearers. In fact, information garnered through exegesis can help the hearer to discern that events surrounding the text are also contemporaneous to the present. Thus, exegesis could help bridge the gap separating the past from the present.

Before we go further in trying to gasp what the exegetical process entails, a look at some pertinent terms will help to shed some light. Greek legend says that there were two beings who were messengers of the gods. One was Interpress, whose role was to interpret the messages of the gods to humans. The other was Hermes, a wing-footed messenger who carried messages between the gods and humans.[20] From their two names come the two words *interpretation* and *hermeneutics*. The word *exegesis* has its roots in Greek language in which the prefix *ex* means "out of" and *exegeisthai*, from which *exegesis* comes, means "to show the way out of." The terms combine to mean "getting meaning out of the text." Hermeneutics sets the principles and guidelines as a theoretical approach that shows how to get the message from the Bible. The results of exegesis accomplish the hermeneutical process.[21] Hermeneutics aims at connecting the biblical text and contemporary contextual life in a relevant way. Hermeneutical interpretation is a process of peeling off the ancient wrappings of the biblical text and letting it be understood afresh in a given contemporary and contextual setting.

Exegesis is a crucial step in the preparation of a sermon but it is not limited to meeting the needs of the preacher. In fact, scholars who give detailed attention to exegesis are not in most cases preachers. Instead, preachers benefit tremendously from the fruits of these exegetes. It is important for the preacher to be aware that there is exegesis for academic pursuit to have a comprehensive grasp of the text, and exegesis for the purpose of communicating the gospel. We shall elaborate and illustrate this distinction later. Exegesis is a question-driven exercise that can lead to this principle: The more pertinent questions one asks the more he or she understands the complex dimensions of the biblical text. Questions may be formulated to solicit information on the author, purpose of writing, date of authorship, the socioeconomic and political milieu of the time, the composition of the audience, literary genre under which the text falls, classification of language forms used, and many more.

An illustration for the Zimbabwe situation that can be adapted for any context with similar events or historical episodes is appropriate. Imagine that two thousand years from today someone comes across the words *chef* and *povo* in a book about Shona or Ndebele culture written in 1982. The preacher will likely sense that the words *chef* and *povo* are not part of the vocabulary of the Ndebele or Shona ethnic languages. In the process of finding their meanings and how they got into Zimbabwean culture, the reader traces the words to the Portuguese language and finally to Mozambique. In reading other books on the history of Zimbabwe, our reader becomes aware that Zimbabweans waged a war of liberation from bases in Mozambique, leading to independence in 1980. A study of the meaning of the words in Portuguese show that *chef* means boss or someone in position of leadership and authority and *povo* means the ordinary people who look up to the *chefs* or those in authority for direction and leadership. Equipped with such historical meaning and background the reader is now more informed to understand that passage in the Shona or Ndebele book on culture. The reader exegeted the passage in that book. Of course this is a simplified version of a complex process, but this example is close to the actual process followed in exegesis.

Regarding the distinction between exegesis for preaching and that done to satisfy the inquisitive mind of the scholar, exegesis for preaching is done to satisfy their hermeneutic quests on the text and is selective in nature. Understanding the text for the purpose of preaching is not only a cerebral task. The reader allows the text to induce some emotions in him or her.[22] Again, an illustration might be helpful in differentiating the two processes. As we read the parable of the Prodigal Son (Luke 15:11–32), exegesis will tell us that for a Jew, feeding swine and contemplating eating the same food as hogs or pigs were degrading. Reading that the father ran to meet his son indicates the urgency of the situation to Africans, because this is not expected of adults, especially in the Zimbabwean culture.

The exegete may also learn that it was not unusual for the father to distribute his inheritance among his sons while he was still alive. Let us imagine that the exegesis yields information about the number of pigs the son was likely to feed, their required weight before they could be sold at the market, and all sorts of detailed information. The task for the preacher is to select only that information that is likely to have a direct purpose in communicating the gospel. In our example, the weight of the pigs and the number one could feed is irrelevant for the purpose of preaching. But to know that the father ran to show his eagerness to meet his son is worthwhile. Exegesis for preaching raises the question of application of the text to the contemporary situation.

One more word about hermeneutics is that there is no meaning of a biblical text that should be held as the telos for all times and people in all contexts. Biblical scholarship recently has witnessed the emergence of a hermeneutics of suspicion as regards feminist reading and exegesis of the Bible. Feminists have successfully detected and expected the male view as the undergirding perspective in biblical interpretation. It is in that light that I urge the African exegete to approach the text with scrutiny motivated by a heightened sense of suspicion on the nature and scope of images, feelings, and experiences that become the repository reservoir of interpretation.

The African exegete must inquire about the text while wearing African lenses and cultural identity. The African should not tremble at the mention of *eisegesis*, which is reading one's own meaning into the text, because all preaching has some elements of eisegesis if the text is to speak to people's experiences. While not openly endorsing eisegesis in the interpretation of the text, Fred B. Craddock cautioned against a form of rigid straightjacket approach to the exegesis of the text. While fear of eisegesis should be upheld, it should also be understood that a clear grasp of the existential situation adds flesh and texture to the meaning of the text.[23] "Sensitivity to the concrete issues of one's own time," said Craddock, "increases sensitivity to the issues of the text contributing positively to the understanding of the passage of scripture."[24]

The Sermon Outline

Now that the preacher has a text that has yielded some thoughts through reflection and exegesis, added to that some material garnered from study and observation, the next step is to develop an outline that imposes order on the gathered information around the sermon idea. A sermon outline is the skeleton around which the flesh of the message is attached. An outline helps the preacher see what comes first, which illustration must be included and at what point in the sermon, and how much material must be allocated under a subheading. It helps determine the smooth progression and development of the sermon ideas proportionate to each segment.

Different types of sermon outlines have been thoroughly discussed and exemplified in readily accessible sources and I do not intend to repeat them here.[25] To give an example, we can have a question-based outline: Who is Jesus Christ? Why did he come? What could we do with him? What are the consequences of not doing anything with him? I have in mind a sermon based on the question Pilate asked, "Then what shall I do with Jesus who is called Christ?" (Matt. 27:22). Sermon outlines generally develop from the biblical text itself, although there should be flexibility to do what is natural to the purpose of the sermon. The three-point sermon outline still lives but it is no longer the norm. The content and available time will influence the nature of an outline.

A point to note however is that a sermon outline that demands meticulous attention from the preacher is foreign in the oral speaking tradition of the Africans. Any detectable outline in the chief's or elder's speech surfaces as a natural feature of that particular speech rather than as a result of deliberate effort. Traditional African speech was based on lived experiences and sustained by cultural wisdom through proverbs, idioms, and other forms of rhetoric. An outline implies that the speaker will refer to it to keep on track because the subject is relatively new. With lived experiences, the speech is absorbed and becomes part of the being of the speaker and therefore there is no need of an outline. Further, African speech is mostly conversational rather than argumentative. The goal is not to score points but to reach consensus and bring the rest on board. This consensus-oriented rhetoric is more evident at the chief's court where cases are tried.[26] In a conversation one is not get preoccupied with outlines. In addition, the pattern of speech making is more or less characterized by uniformity. The African speaker usually begins by making a conscious effort to build rapport with the listeners, and then says what must be said, while always checking to see if the audience is still listening. Such a familiar pattern meant that there was no need of an outline.

Maybe what M. Bloch found about the political speeches of the Merina of Madagascar contain some elements applicable to other African contexts. A Merina speaker begins by expressing how unworthy he/she is to speak at such a gathering. The idea is to be polite and unpresumptuous before others. Then the speech unfolds by referring to widely accepted values in the community, so that people's views will coalesce into a point of agreement. Then the intended idea is presented couched in appropriate proverbs meant to bolster the proposal. A moment of silence follows, indicating that the audience has accepted the speaker and the message.[27] Such a well-traveled path in speech making does not require an outline.

Based on what I observed in the chief's court in my home village at Gandanzara, another reason for not needing an outline is that African traditional speeches are short and to the point. Forget about modern Westernized speech making, which can last for more than an hour. The traditional African speech is brief because it involves conversation and dialogue to allow listeners to give their input along the way. Speech making as a lengthy monologue is not common in African traditional culture.

Probably more than any other reason for not relying on an outline is the fact that the traditional form of communication in Africa is oral. An outline to which the speaker could refer presupposes a culture of written communication. Even in today's Africa, the written word plays second fiddle to the spoken word. When homileticians, especially those in the West, urge preachers to preach without notes, is it not an indirect affirmation of the African traditional way of speech making? In the end what matters is whether the preacher can make sense of the material and have an internalized order to enable him or her and the listeners to follow in the most natural manner possible. There is a proverb in Shona that says, "*Mbudzi kudya mufenje kutodza mai*" (for a goat to eat leaves of a certain tree it is imitating its mother). African preachers will do better to learn from their oral traditional culture and use outlines only as subordinate aids to their sermon making and delivery.

Leave No Stone Unturned

When the sermon is ready, the next step is planning the delivery. There are two stages of delivering a sermon—the preparatory delivery practice and the actual delivery of the sermon. The decision to take into the pulpit a full written sermon or scant notes or no notes is made at this stage.

The preacher should not take for granted that all the hard work and inspiration will lead to a smooth delivery. Practicing the sermon beforehand will be helpful in spotting potential problems. There is no need to think that such practice turns preaching into a performance. Pre-delivery preparations will not add or subtract anything from the art of preaching. Practicing something with the aim of perfecting it does not mean you believe less in what you are doing. It is better to adjust distracting or unhelpful traits before you are in the pulpit. With the passage of time and experience the preacher can comfortably skip this practice.

If the preacher is an invited guest, it is advisable to be at the sanctuary before the time of the service to become acquainted with the setup. A number of African congregations do not fit in their sanctuaries, so some of the people sit outside. Arriving early allows time to gauge how to project your voice to reach everyone. Where a microphone is provided, have the technician set it up and check its efficiency. If you occasionally move out of the pulpit to reach out to the congregation (as most African preachers like to do), then check to see if this is possible.

How does a preacher know that he or she is prepared? According to Fred B. Craddock, "In the final analysis, adequacy of preparation is not consistently evidenced by how much paper, if any, one carries into the pulpit. Rather, readiness to preach is demonstrated by certainty of theme and purpose and clear movement toward one's goal with serious delight."[28] In the same vein, H. Beecher Hicks pointed out that the process of taking the material from the study to do what was intended in the pulpit is a complex issue for every preacher. "The authentic preacher," said Hicks, "comes to the pulpit unsure if the bones can live. He can only respond to the question by saying, 'Lord God, thou knowest'."[29] As in the analogy about safety precautions in an aircraft at the beginning of this chapter, preparing to preach should be undertaken with the assurance that it is unlikely that the Holy Spirit will let anything go wrong.

Chapter 2

What Do You Preach? The Message

The mystery about preaching is that there is nothing inherently new about the message and yet people continually return to hear that same message. For the individual worshipper the hope is that this one more time the message will have a new meaning. One cannot explain this recurrent urge to hear the same message apart from what Jesus Christ told us, "It is written, 'Man shall not live by bread alone, but by every word that proceeds from the mouth of God'" (Matt. 4:4). This is the hunger for the Word of God that led Augustine to declare that his soul could not rest until he rested in God.[1]

Indeed, the message is the same, but only in that Jesus Christ, crucified and risen from the dead, is preached. This does not rule out the diversity with which this message is communicated in various circumstances and contexts. In some cases, the message of Jesus Christ assures and affirms. In other cases, the message of Jesus Christ comforts those who are heavy laden and promises them rest. That Jesus Christ is incarnate in every conceivable context keeps this seemingly same message relevant and meaningful to all people at all times. With Christ as the center of it all, the gospel message for Africa nevertheless should focus on some aspects germane to the African situation for it to be meaningful. Contextualizing the preached message can be done in any part of the world where Jesus Christ is preached.

Recognizing the need of a contextualized message does not mean we sideline general maxims about preaching. It still behooves every African preacher to aim at preaching "the whole counsel of God."[2] Further, the preached message is more important in any form of communication than the method of delivery.[3] When making a case for the contextualization of the gospel, African theologians focus on the mode of communication rather than on new ways of articulating the gospel amenable to and commensurate with African culture.[4] African theologians should stretch their minds and face the urgent need now for a gospel especially molded and packaged for Africa. It is my attempt in this chapter to show the need for a contextualized message, not only the inculturated modes of preaching. This chapter will also deal with other essentials that are part of the preached message in any situation.

The Preached Message and the Congregation

The nature and scope of the message depends on the understanding of a given congregation. Each congregation within the Christian faith has its stages and development patterns. There are likes and dislikes, fears and doubts, strengths and weaknesses that in the end influence the extent and depth of the preached message. Hear St. Paul: "I fed you with milk, not solid food; for you were not ready for it, and even yet you are not ready" (1 Cor. 3:2). This metaphorical expression can be applied to any congregation where people are not growing in their faith. A congregation that has not taken seriously "Repent, for the kingdom of heaven is at hand" will retard the progress toward being fed other "solid food" of the gospel (Matt. 3:2). At the same time there are congregations who beg the preacher not to pander to the likes and self-seeking interests of the hearers.[5] First and foremost, the gospel raises the Cross before the congregation and then the Resurrection follows. Joy always follows the Cross whose continued presence is a reality for all times in all contexts.[6]

A prepared message for the congregation can have different purposes, but most of all it should bring comfort and encouragement. As Austin Phelps said, "If there is one thing more obvious than another in the general strain of apostolic preaching, it is the preponderance of words of encouragement over those of reproof and commination."[7] The essence of the Christian faith is an optimistic view of life that infuses the human heart with hope.[8] In the African context where people live with unpredictable and ever-changing socioeconomic and political circumstances, the gospel message should emphasize pastoral care and compassion. I believe that all preaching needs to have a pastoral component to it. Without that element, building the community of God becomes difficult. I am speaking of pastoral preaching as "an attempt to meet the individual and personal needs of the people by means of a sermon," as Charles F. Kemp says.[9] For each message to be meaningful it must engage the individual's concerns, hence all effective preaching is pastoral. The African preacher is called upon to view the congregation with compassion. Indeed, "the way the pastor views his congregation," said Kemp, "will largely determine his own attitudes, the content of his message, even his tone of voice."[10]

By a pastoral message for Africa we do not mean pie in heaven. It is instead the gospel of presence where Jesus Christ promises to stand with the woman who has been deserted by her husband and left alone to fend for herself and her children. It is a message that comforts a man whose whole family has been decimated in the civil war. This pastoral message also is extended to those who are unemployed and whose prospects for the future are bleak. The Jesus Christ preached in Africa should say something hopeful about these complex socioeconomic issues and to the despair they create.

A pastoral message should persuade listeners "to change their lives for the better."[11] This is a noble focus for a preacher, but African social and political institutions can stultify efforts individuals make to try to live better lives. We need a holistic approach to the message, one that addresses the whole person both physically and spiritually. Inasmuch as Africans find solace in momentary spiritual uplifting through the message, preachers must not settle only for these episodic spiritual flights. There is nothing wrong in experiencing emotions in worship; the problem comes when such experiences become the purpose of the message. Africa is in need of messages that encourage people to transform what they hear into practical guidelines for life in the here and the hereafter. As one author put it, a sermon should not be like delivering a lecture on medicine to sick people. What the sick people need is the medicine itself.[12] Rather than solely disseminating information, the message must articulate the essence of how God acts in Jesus Christ.[13]

For the African congregation the message must be full of "*re* words, renew, rebirth, restore, remake, reconcile."[14] Like any other people, Africans long for a message that remakes them anew in the face of disintegrative forces of evil.

African people feel under threat of real and imagined forces of evil. As Henry H. Mitchell put it, "Only positive truths about God through Christ give healing and empowerment, causing great rejoicing and praise. The more people rejoice about the goodness and faithfulness of God, the more they establish that joyous quality or atmosphere in the psychic space of their lives, regardless of outer chaos."[15]

Elements of the Preached Message for Africa

In the preceding section we have discussed the tone the message from the African pulpit should assume. Our purpose now is to propose what preaching the gospel message of Jesus Christ should entail. In his research on preaching in Malawi, Ross found that the message is usually abstract with no real focus on the pressing existential issues of life. There is little focus on the family or society as a whole. Instead, preaching addresses personal morality.[16] It is important to preach about personal morality, but preaching against adultery and general promiscuity, stealing, hatred, drunkenness, pride, jealousy, lying, and so forth is not enough.[17] The message preached in Zimbabwean churches also often aims at improving personal morality. Preachers may gain ground when they realize that the sins against which they warn their people should be viewed in light of the prevailing socioeconomic and political milieu. It is common to hear sex workers in Zimbabwe boasting in the media that it is better to die from AIDS than to die from hunger. This is not a self-indicting statement but a critique of the poverty in Zimbabwe that drives people into such suicidal behavior. For the majority these sins are a means of survival.

The message for Africa cannot continue to be limited to the idea of salvation for the individual, "who is called to renounce himself, and to adopt certain attitudes and to flee the influence of his environment while preparing to leave for Heaven and to expect the end of this age."[18] There is a strong tendency among African preachers and the people to use the gospel as an escape from the realities of this world. The future is viewed as the dawn of the end of the world. The world as a transient space is highlighted.[19] "There is much interest in paradise" as a spiritual entity rather than a concrete existential goal to attain.[20] Such defeatist attitudes explain why Africa is fertile for planting and expansion of doomsday cults and other religious sects with dubious teachings. If the energy of spiritual and emotional expression can be balanced with realistic reflection on what must be done to improve one's environment in concrete and active ways, then the religious ferment in Africa can be for the good of the whole person.

What specific elements in the preached message for Africa can balance emotionalism with the realism of life? First, the message from the African pulpit should express the need for community. Community is a biblical concept as well as a vivid characteristic of traditional African culture. As former president of South Africa Nelson Mandela once said, he felt he cast his first vote not alone but with those gone before him.[21] Despite the pressures brought about by industrialization and urbanization, Africans should resist a lifestyle based on unbridled individualism. The response Cain gave to the Lord after murdering his brother Abel, "I do not know; am I my brother's keeper?" (Gen. 4:9b), is not for the African. It is the responsibility of the African preacher to remind the people that their moral strength lies in being accountable to their brothers and sisters.

Africans express a sense of presence and being within the community. They do not regard time just being with each other as wasted. As one missionary perceptively noted, "The two-to three-hour worship services Africans enjoy; their way of relaxing by just being in each others company, not waiting for anything; and their lengthy, polite greeting formulas—all speak of a culture that puts accomplishment in a place secondary to living."[22] It does not make sense for the African pastor to lead worship as a means of building a community of believers and yet refrain from preaching a community-oriented message. Although we teach in seminaries the value of *koinonia* groups and covenant agreements, these practices emerging from the West do not have much to teach Africans about the meaning of communal life.

Community thrives upon a smooth flow of communication and when people have time for each other. Some of the stresses Africans suffer are a result of lack of time. Africans measure time as it relates to meeting human needs more so than in terms of being busy. I don't think that Jesus Christ was carefree to the point of not having a daily schedule. Nevertheless, we see that expressions of compassion and care took precedence over whatever he might set out to do. Many Africans are late for scheduled meetings because they meet a friend or a relative along the way and chat a bit out of courtesy. They do not feel bad about being late. In fact, simply passing that person in a hurry to get to the meeting on time may bother him to her as wrong. This is not to say that Africans today can ignore the demands of time. My point is that the preached message should help African listeners to value time spent in the company of others as crucial to upholding community.

I attended a convocation in the United States several years ago (25–26 Feb. 2000) on "Raising the Banner: Reclaiming the Village." The purpose of the convocation was to "provide a forum to discuss and form a plan of action that can result in favorable and helpful relations among youth, in families and communities."[23] Topics focused on the family and the village as vital aspects of community life. The theme of the convocation shows the emerging awareness among African-Americans for reclaiming the roots they share in the African heritage of community. It is therefore incumbent on the African preacher to extol the values of life based on community. To preach with an eye on community is to live up to the church's expectation that the message should form the community.[24]

Another topic that African preaching should address with care but urgently is superstition. I say with care because simply castigating a system of belief without carefully weighing the dimensions of the subject might exacerbate the problem. Through superstitious beliefs people expose themselves to cheats and lose money and property in the process. In some cases superstition hinders progress as people value magic over hard work. Superstitious beliefs are a hindrance to the government, non-governmental agencies, and the church itself in their efforts to reduce the spread of HIV and AIDS.

At a former mining settlement near Bindura in Zimbabwe, deaths caused by AIDS-related complications were blamed on witchcraft. A 22-year-old man blamed evil spirits for his sickness. Although his mother and wife were reportedly aware that their ill health was AIDS-related, they did not tell the young man. "My wife has been ill for close to a year, and before she had two miscarriages. We have now found a good traditional healer who is capable of exorcising the evil spirits troubling them," he said.[25] These traditional healers are cashing in on unsuspecting patients.

In the same paper as the article on AIDS there was a report about a white commercial farmer who called a *n'anga* to exorcise his farming community. The owner of the farm called a traditional healer who supposedly unearthed a host of hair-raising items: owls, snakes, goblins, and human body parts, including a male sex organ. The *n'anga* said that the objects were used to cause mysterious illnesses and death to perceived enemies. "We took the measures because we had been observing the problem of witchcraft for quite some time and since I know the people and their tradition I called in the *n'anga*. I hope the move will improve morale on the farm," said the owner.[26]

African preachers must tackle issues that if left to thrive will impact negatively on the well-being of the community. Community life is not built on suspicious foundations of mistrust of one another. Jealousy, laziness, and gossip are some of the evils that lead to superstition. At one time, there was a superstitious belief that someone with magical powers could take crops from another's field and transfer them to his and increase the yield. The use of *diwisi*, as the magic is called, supposedly caused other peasant farmers to have poor harvests. This belief retarded agricultural development because instead of improving soil fertility through adding manure and other means, people wished they had *diwisi*. This is no longer much of a problem with African farmers.

This is an example of a problem the African preacher should confront and address. The evils that affect Africans are both personal and extend into the social fabric of the community. As Mugambi noted, Christianity can have a message of development and hope, and at the same time focus on a personal message of building character and offering a way out to those who are lonely or caught up in family problems.[27] African preachers need to address a personal message of salvation as well as a message of comprehensive redemption for the whole person.

Further, prophetic message should be a key element in African preaching. A strong and authentic prophetic message draws its inspiration from a prophetic theology. Writing in the context of apartheid South Africa, John W. de Gruchy described the distinctions between different theologies at the time of formulating the Kairos Document. State theology undergirded the apartheid socio-economic political system; church theology was against apartheid but virtually incapable of transforming the state; and prophetic theology was critical of apartheid and called upon the church to witness to and engage the state in transformative change.[28] While the theology in African churches is more often than not incapable of ushering in practical transformative results in people's lives, we know as evidenced by the church in South Africa that pulpit messages in African churches can be transformative.

In her book, *Preaching as Weeping, Confession, and Resistance: Radical Responses to Radical Evil,* Christine M. Smith, identified three worldviews of preaching: the world of the text, the preacher's and community's world where preaching takes place, and the world of society at large. Preaching can easily show a particular bias toward one of the worldviews at the expense of the others. Smith pointed out that preaching often focuses more on the world of the preacher than on the larger society.[29]

This is true for Zimbabwe and much of Africa. At a revival organized by women of The United Methodist Church, a preacher preached on relationships between mothersin-law and their daughters-in-law. The sermon rightly responded to cases of strained relationships between the two. Instead of approaching the issue from a larger social context, the preacher issued advisory statements urging the daughters-in-law to be agreeable with their mothers-in-law. No attention was given to the issue of generation gap or to the socioeconomic changes that have uprooted young couples from rural areas to the cities away from their families. Although this sermon addressed the problem, a prophetic message would recognize the relationship problems and examine the issues that affect this relationship.

Christine Smith went on to explain that preaching is figuratively synonymous to weeping because it is characterized by deep passionate feeling in the face of widespread suffering in the world.[30] There is a lot of weeping in African churches but the source is more likely self-pity and other personal problems than concern for the suffering of people in society at large. "Preachers," said Smith, "are often better at describing a world they hope for than articulating truth about the real world."[31]

Preaching is directed to the community of believers to enable them to live a life characterized by "a distinctive identity in the world."[32] Or to put it differently, "preaching is usually done in and to the church. The church is a set of people who are already called out by previous preaching."[33] But for the African church the challenge is to extend and widen the catchment area for the Word. One way is to see listeners as people existing in the larger society. The message of preaching should address the congregation as people who are both redeemed and redeeming. This redemption that people have experienced in the church through Jesus Christ is to be shared with others.

The people themselves show an awareness of the role of the church to raise a prophetic voice. A cartoon appeared in a Zimbabwean independent newspaper with the heading, "A Deafening Silence . . ." In it, there were three clergy persons, one holding ears with a caption, "Hear no evil," one holding the mouth with the words, "Speak no evil," and a third one holding eyes with accompanying words, "See no evil." At the other end was a scene depicting the violence among political parties in Zimbabwe as the nation prepared for national parliamentary elections for 2000.[34] Another independent paper more directly called upon the church in Zimbabwe to speak against politically motivated violence that threatened the peace of the nation.[35]

"It is the speech of the prophet that must be heard in the pulpit of the free," said G. Bromley Oxman. "It must be declaratory of the will of God: thus says the Lord."[36] From the pulpit must flow the message of judgment, justice, and moral conduct, in daring specific terms. Gardner C. Taylor used the image of a watchman for the preacher. The role of a watchman is to scan the forests and hills and warn the people of the advancing enemy. Because the watchman's life is at risk, there is also a sense of urgency.[37] When the church fails in its duty as a watchman, the people suffer at the hands of marauding Satan. I am haunted by the report that during the massacre in Rwanda, people sought refuge in the church buildings but were followed and murdered there. The symbolism of the incident depicts a powerless church in Africa. To be sure, the church has played a significant role in ending the civil war and bringing peace in Mozambique and in putting pressure on the apartheid government in South Africa, but it must do more as a prophetic voice in independent Africa.

In assessing what Martin Luther King, Jr., viewed as the prophetic message in a sermon, Richard Lischer noted that "if the sermon is promoting the kinds of liberation and love that God-in-Jesus has been known to sponsor in the Bible and if it is opposing the kinds of injustice that God has always hated, then the sermon is the word of God and its preacher is a genuine prophet."[38] Basically then a prophetic message is true to the teachings of God as revealed through Jesus Christ in the Bible. Instead of merely engaging in "a profession of prohibitions" in their preaching, African preachers must tell the people how they can live creatively.[39] It is through the prophetic message that people will expand their outlook on life and live it abundantly as promised in the gospel. Finally, it is incumbent on every preacher to know that as Markquart pointed out, "The roots of the office of preaching are found in the prophets. These men and women were rooted and grounded in God's word and will and they spoke God's word and will to the world in which they lived. We preachers need to have the courage to do the same."[40] This is the clarion call for the African preacher.

Preach a Biblical and Theological Message

To further attempt to answer the question about what must be preached, we call the preacher's attention to the need to preach a biblically and theologically based message. The elements of the message discussed in the preaching segments so far are not outside the realm of the Bible and theology. The attempt here is to convince African preachers of the need for sermons to be grounded in the Bible and developed on sound theological convictions. True Christian theology finds rationale for its themes and conclusions ultimately from the Bible. However, we mention the two poles, biblical and theological, to emphasize their complementary relationship in the development of the preached message.

"Reading the sermon outlines," observed Kenneth R. Ross, "left me with the impression that, were it not for the Christmas and Easter seasons, there would be relatively little emphasis on Christ himself."[41] This observation about preaching in Malawi is not confined to that place. In 1999, I was invited as a guest preacher by another circuit and I missed our church's Easter service. When I came back, a colleague told me how disappointing it was to listen to an Easter sermon where there was no focus on Jesus Christ. The guest preacher invited at our church apparently did not refer to Jesus Christ in a way that satisfied my friend. Preaching by all means must be Christocentric in nature and focus. Centering one's preaching on Jesus Christ is first and foremost when preaching biblically and theologically.

The preacher of the gospel is a theologian who stands within a long established tradition. There are basic beliefs about Jesus Christ, God, the meaning of the church as a gathered community of believers, the nature of humanity in God's creation, and sin and forgiveness that must be shared in depth with the congregation. As Elizabeth Achtemeier urged, preachers should develop a Christian theology that becomes part of one's being and that theology should guide and give counsel to every sermon preached.[42]

For theology to accomplish its mission it must inform the gathered church of the scope and nature of several key themes. The kingdom of God should be one of the central themes in preaching. Jesus Christ came preaching the kingdom of God. Today, denominations that follow the lectionary come across the season of the Kingdomtide. Preachers can help congregations see the clear call in the Lord's Prayer for the kingdom of God to come on earth. What are the implications for preaching that call for the will of God to happen on earth as it is in heaven? How do Africans preach in the context of devastating hunger in neighboring African countries? Existential preaching acknowledges what goes on in people's lives. The African preacher in the tradition of the prophet continually faces the challenges of preaching the gospel of the kingdom of God.

Another major biblical and theological theme is the love of God as revealed to us through Jesus Christ. Love has many dimensions. One dimension is the love between husband and wife, which is valid and necessary. But preachers in Africa should also focus on sacrificial love, an essential attribute of God's love. This love demands self-giving and is based on grace and not on the law. While the Bible narrates incidents in which Jesus Christ castigated Pharisees and other religious leaders, much of the gospel is simply compassionate love. The preacher must not preach only what people want to hear. At times they need to be warned and cautioned about sin. But when all that has been said, "It is not the purpose of Christian preaching to send a congregation away every Sunday with nothing more than a bad conscience. We are called to be heralds of grace, not midwives of calamity."[43]

Last but not least, preaching today exists because Jesus Christ rose from the dead. St. Paul raised this awareness about the centrality of the Resurrection in no uncertain terms. "If Christ has not been raised, then our preaching is in vain and your faith is in vain" (1 Cor. 15:14), he declared. Every Sunday should be celebrated as Resurrection Sunday. "Indeed, our powerlessness in preaching the gospel stems from our failure to realize that the Christian life is lived in Lent," lamented T. D. Niles.[44] Preaching devoid of the message of the Resurrection is surely powerless and cannot in turn empower the audience. Africa needs an empowering message that derives its content and inspiration from the Resurrection of Jesus Christ.

The Message for Different Occasions

A student once asked me if I could include in the syllabus of the course I taught information on how to preach on different occasions such as weddings and funerals. This is a legitimate concern for students of preaching and many preachers. I intend to give a few guidelines that can be used whenever a situation to preach on a specific occasion arises. Then we will select a few specific occasions for a more detailed explanation.

First, every sermon is for a specific occasion in the sense that each worship setting is unique. Second, other specific occasions are inherent in the Christian year. A preacher who follows the lectionary will have more distinct occasions to preach on. Third, other special occasions in preaching come from recognizing memorial days and other days that are celebrated by the community or by the nation. For example, this could include a Sunday marking the establishment of a local church or national independence day.

Fourth, the preacher can be resourceful and create new days for specific sermons. Churches in Zimbabwe have a special Harvest Sunday on which people give gifts to God in thanksgiving for the blessings they have received. In African traditional culture, prayers and festivals were offered during the planting season. A local church could have a planting Sunday in which different seeds could be brought to church for specific prayers of dedication. This may be more suitable for rural churches and a sermon for such a day could be developed.

Fifth, whenever faced with the task of preaching on a special occasion the preacher and the congregation need to understand the meaning of the event and how it relates to the worship service. How does God speak through Jesus Christ to a people confronted with such an event in their lives? Is there any specific theological understanding pertaining to the event that the preacher must understand and base the sermon on?

Sixth, a sermon on a specific occasion should focus on that event. Make it so specific that anyone would know what the worshippers are celebrating just by hearing the sermon. Seventh, the preacher whose sermons are geared for specific occasions will need access to appropriate biblical texts. Resource books such as *Nave's Topical Bible* and others will be helpful. In the African situation the preacher may have to contact seminary libraries and make a special trip to get such resources. One could make a collection of biblical texts on a variety of topics for future use.

Eighth, the preacher should make the congregation aware in advance about the forthcoming worship event. If the congregation is not informed and not prepared the preacher's sermon will not be heard and received with a sense of expectation by the listeners. Ninth, most special occasions require that the regular pastor should preach rather than a guest preacher. For an occasion when focused preparation is needed, the pastor is the best choice for the task. Tenth, in some cases sermons should be brief to allow time for people to actively participate in the event. Africans like to do things together in community. Festivals are popular with African congregations and hence adequate time should be allocated for active participation.

We shall now examine a few special occasions for preaching and show how the above guidelines are applicable. In preaching and in pastoral work as a whole, a pastor will benefit from being imaginative and resourceful.

Sacraments and Lectionary-Related Events

Denominations have different understandings of sacraments but here I have in mind baptism and Holy Communion. Even the name *Holy Communion* is not commonly used by all denominations. I urge that the pastor be well informed about the teaching of the universal Church and what holds for a particular denomination. Other denominations celebrate Holy Communion every Sunday and on other occasions such as at weddings or funerals. Some denominations celebrate Holy Communion on specific Sundays in the month or monthly and so forth. For those churches that celebrate Holy Communion only occasionally, it can be important to focus the whole sermon on it.

My observation is that celebrating Holy Communion sometimes is done as an appendage to the sermon. At times, all the preacher does is refer in passing to the table for a sermon that was wholly focused on something else. My specific experience in The United Methodist

Church in Zimbabwe is that Holy Communion celebrated on Maundy Thursday for Passion Week is given special focus and attention.

But all Holy Communion celebrations have their roots in the one that Jesus Christ celebrated as the Last Supper in Jerusalem the night he was betrayed. When done with full understanding of the far-reaching implications of the event for the Christian life, Holy Communion is an acted sermon that surpasses any homily one could ever preach. Here is an occasion where the congregation participates by receiving the body and the blood of Christ that was given for them. Preaching itself should not take a predominant position; instead give more time to the actual celebration of the event.

In The United Methodist Church and in other churches, we dismiss the people after receiving communion with quotes from the scriptures or other inspired words. People listen carefully because this word is for this particular group kneeling in front. Such a practice is abandoned whenever time has been spent on the sermon and other things. There is also the practice of calling individuals by name when they receive the elements. This can be particularly meaningful. If the pastor cannot remember every name, the recipient can say his or her first name for the pastor to call out and then give the communion. All these suggestions highlight the need to make Holy Communion and not the sermon the central focus for that particular worship service.

The same is the true for baptism, another crucial sacrament in the church. On the day of the baptism the congregation should take special interest in the event and all worship should be developed around it. This is again different for denominations that baptize almost every Sunday. But for those who set specific days for baptism, it is important that the sermon is based on the event.

Both the preacher and the congregation should understand the biblical and theological meaning of Holy Communion and baptism. Some denominations have their own theologians who help guide the church in understanding theological issues. When the preacher is informed, the sermon can be built on a theologically sound foundation. There are numerous themes the preacher could focus on. These could include the meaning of Holy Communion or baptism and how each relates to contemporary Christian life. This may be too large a subject for one sermon, and can be broken into units for multiple sermons. A sermon on baptism could focus on the biblical teaching of baptism as dying with Jesus Christ or union with Christ. On Holy Communion one could focus on the sacrificial thrust, thanksgiving, and other themes.

We assume that the preacher has a repertoire of biblical texts on these subjects and has followed the recommended steps in preparing to preach. Preachers sometime think that because they have preached often on baptism or Holy Communion there is no need of exegesis. The truth is that baptism and Holy Communion are communicated in the Bible through texts loaded with imagery far removed from our contemporary understanding and experience.

Sometimes preachers do not focus their sermons on baptism and Holy Communion because these are doctrines. I have observed and heard from preachers that doctrinal preaching is not the focus of Africans in Zimbabwe and one could probably say the same for other African countries. Even at Easter it is common to go through the whole season without hearing a solid sermon on the doctrine of atonement or forgiveness. Preachers mention that we have been saved by the blood of Jesus Christ and that our sins have been forgiven, but don't explain how such salvation and forgiveness have been effected. The same applies to special lectionary days such as Pentecost, Epiphany, Ash Wednesday, and Christmas. Sermons often miss the relevant content based on a fair grasp of these events. Since Africans already use ashes for healing and for some other rituals, a preacher could make use of such traditions to make worship on Ash Wednesday more meaningful. Because in Zimbabwe some Shona people sprinkle ashes on their heads when mourning a close relative or a spouse, using ashes on Ash Wednesday could be more understandable.

If a child beats a parent he or she has to go away (*kutiza botso*) from home wearing a sackcloth before reconciliation could be possible. This practice in Shona culture blends well with the biblical texts on using ashes and wearing sackcloth. Being oblivious of one's context sometimes causes African preachers to depend heavily on meanings imposed by Westerners who are far removed from having an authentic understanding of these practices. Since commentaries do not discuss African experiences on these and other texts, African preachers need to create their own interpretation of African cultural practices.

Pentecost is an ideal time for preachers to relate the sermon to the spiritual ferment that characterizes African life. This is the time to develop sermons on the work and manifestations of the Holy Sprit. Such sermons could counter some misguided doctrines that are creeping into the church. The church in Africa must pray for the coming of the Holy Spirit upon the people as part of its ministry and legitimate expectation.

Weddings

For weddings, the sermon develops as a result of the relationship the pastor has with the marriage partners. Pre-marital pastoral conversations and counseling set the stage for sermons that are personal and meaningful to the couple.

Weddings in Africa draw large crowds and this gives the pastor opportunity to preach to some people who seldom come to church. The sermon could focus on the renewal of marriage vows for older couples. This is the time for the church to claim and emphasize the covenant between God and the marriage partners.

In Zimbabwe some young couples see the extended family as a burden. When someone says the house is full of E. F., this means full of the extended family. Given the economic hardships of most African people, it is understandable that the burden of caring for family becomes heavy for young people starting a family. Still the gospel that upholds community values and sharing must be preached. I usually remind young couples at their weddings that economic hardships are not an excuse to avoid giving to and sharing with one's family. In Shona a popular saying is, "*Ukama igasva hunodzadziswa nekudya*," which means, "Relationship is incomplete until the relatives share and eat together." In other words, eating together is the one act that consolidates relationships. People generally receive these sermons warmly because of the attempt to contextualize marriage in African culture.

In African churches every opportunity, even a wedding, is used for evangelism and to bring new souls to Christ. Sometimes the preacher will mistakenly pay more attention to those who have come to the church for the first time and ignore the marriage partners. As we have said earlier, preaching for special occasions should reflect and be meaningful to that event. The sermon should be as personal as the preacher can make it.

In urban areas it is now common for the sermon and the whole ceremony to be videotaped. This technology captures much of the atmosphere that surrounds the preaching process. It is therefore easier for the couple to listen to the sermon later in a more relaxed mood and pay more attention to the message than they might have done on the actual day. Sermons preached at weddings are likely to be heard by more people beyond the original audience. Thus, it is doubly important for preachers to take all necessary steps in the preparation of a wedding sermon.

Wedding sermons are an ideal example of Fred Craddock's method of preaching that he calls "overhearing the gospel." The approach is based on the premise that people listen to a message with no defenses when they feel that they are not the direct target.[45] People whose marriages are on the verge of breakdown will listen attentively in an environment that is safe for them psychologically. Since the message is not directed at them, they can "overhear the gospel" as it is shared with the wedding couple.

John W. Conway proposed four points to remember in a wedding sermon: First, make it short. Second, let it be personal. Third, be aware of the mystery of marriage. And fourth, address the sermon to the people beyond those directly related to the wedding.[46] In Africa all but the first point are valid. A wedding is a festival and Africans love to celebrate together. It is therefore a mistake to preach a short sermon at an African wedding. It is wise for the pastor to do everything possible to start the ceremony on time so there is adequate time for the sermon. John Conway referred to the Archbishop of Canterbury who preached for three minutes at the wedding of Prince Charles and Lady Diana.[47] But African preachers are better advised to plan to preach not less than fifteen minutes for a short wedding sermon and not more than twenty-five minutes for a regular sermon. Short sermons for a wedding should be the exception rather than the norm.

Funerals

For African pastors preaching at funerals is a regular task. One major reason is that there are still high mortality rates in African countries due to the AIDS pandemic and other life-threatening diseases. Healthcare institutions and services are inadequate to meet the demand. In some remote areas, seriously ill patients are transported to nearby clinics in wheelbarrows because vehicles cannot navigate the bad roads. Malaria still wreaks havoc on the African continent. HIV and AIDS have led to the resurgence of opportunistic diseases such as tuberculosis. As a result, frequent funerals provide a regular platform for preaching to the African preacher.

There are a number of issues an African preacher should bear in mind concerning African funerals. First, African funerals provide avenues through which some traits of African traditional culture and religion are expressed. Strongly held beliefs about what must be done or not done, or what is proper or improper, are shared. Second, an African funeral is a community affair and all community members are expected to attend. Upon hearing of a death, it is appropriate to arrange to be with the bereaved family. The closer you are to the bereaved family and the deceased, the more urgent it is to be at the homestead before the rest of the people.

Third, in African funerals the focus is on being with the bereaved family, not only attending the service and burial. The body is brought home for an overnight vigil, followed by burial the following day. Women spend the night crowded in the room where the coffin is as a way of showing solidarity with the bereaved family. Men sleep in the open air or in tents, if available. Fourth, because of the widespread sense of community, African funerals bring together people of different denominational backgrounds and also those who have no church affiliation.

Fifth, as is my observation in Zimbabwe, funerals can be a source of embarrassment for both the pastor and the bereaved family. Sometimes the deceased was not a church member, but the surviving spouse is an active member and a leader in the church. The preacher then is tempted to compromise by imposing church worship for the funeral. In the African tradition it is hard for the preacher to stay out of the process when the deceased was not a member. The common compromise in some denominations is for the pastor to be present and do everything except the burial ritual.

As with weddings, preaching at a particular funeral should normally be preceded by some relationship or contact between the preacher and the deceased. These contacts could be made during normal life events or by way of visits in the hospital. To be personal when preaching a funeral sermon means being able to interweave the stories from the life of the deceased with the story of the gospel of Jesus Christ. A funeral sermon should say something about the life of the deceased, with a goal of blessing those still living. Some people die after having lived a life with positive accomplishments either in their own Christian growth or in the ways they overtly influenced others for the better. In other cases the preacher has little to draw from the life of the deceased.

Whatever the case might be, it is essential to integrate the life of the deceased into the sermon.

Time the pastor spends listening to the family talk about their loved one can be used to enrich material for the sermon. Africans mourn through monologic speeches, which are reminiscences of the life they lived with the deceased and how the dead person was of immense value to them. Those around may express some affirmations of what is being said to show a sense of togetherness in word and deed. I once had the privilege of speaking at a United Methodist Church pastors' school on the topic, "How can we cope with funerals?" I believe that we can cope by emphasizing the ministry of presence rather than always thinking about what to preach. The bereaved family remembers the pastor not so much for the sermon, but for "what we become to them in this moment of crisis."[48]

L. Arden Almquist has named this African tradition of being there with each other in more expressive terms. He pointed out that "for the Africans, presence is more than merely physical: it has a sacramental character."[49] The Almquist family was a recipient of this gift of silent presence during their missionary work in the Democratic Republic of the Congo, then Zaire, in times of bereavement. The African pastor should not rush to preach but have time to be present with the bereaved family and the rest of the people. The sermon should come as the climax of this expressed act of togetherness.

The gift of the message is hope in the Resurrection of Jesus Christ. The preacher's need to reach the unchurched must not be done at the expense of preaching the essence of the Resurrection of Jesus Christ. A good funeral sermon accentuates why Jesus Christ came, lived, was crucified, died, was buried, and then was raised from the dead.

Another focus for the African preacher is to deal with the concept of the will of God. There is much talk about the will of God in African theological perspective as escapist. As stated earlier, life-threatening diseases are taking a toll on Africans because of lack of health delivery systems. It is incumbent on the African preacher to preach sermons that make people aware of their role in preventing diseases. Sometimes people listen better when they are faced with a death. The larger society should accept responsibility for some of the deaths. The message about the kingdom of God should point not only to going to heaven but also that God's will be done on earth as it is in heaven. When the will of God is done on earth it may mean the development of life-giving and life-sustaining systems for the people.

Preaching at African funerals also can draw from the rich heritage of the belief among Africans in life after death. The preacher should not preach on the Resurrection as if it is a new concept for Africans. Instead, Africans need constant reminders that some biblical truths taught by Jesus Christ are in fact part of their belief system. Contextualization of the Christian faith should focus on ideas and not only on changing forms of worship. The message itself should contain African content, and a funeral sermon provides such an opportunity.

In addition an African funeral is an opportune time for evangelism. It is common for a pastor to preach three or more sermons from the day of death to the time for burial. Prayer meetings where sermons are preached are organized for evenings. The lay preachers and the pastor take turns speaking. No matter how long funeral arrangements take, people should meet for evening prayers at the home of the bereaved up to the day of burial. Such extended time with the bereaved can be valuable for evangelism. The sermon should not use death to frighten people into conversion. It is instead time to show the good life one could live in Jesus Christ and how Christians are people of the promise through the Resurrection of Jesus Christ.

It is also a time for the preacher to notice if superstition arises among the mourners. Africans tend to engage in superstitious talk and speculation after a death. The African preacher should confront the people with a realistic message that recognizes that people die from natural causes. Witch hunting has caused a lot of enmity within

African communities and has broken relationships among relatives in extended families. It is the preacher's privilege to speak against such beliefs in the light of the gospel of Jesus Christ.

In patriarchal African societies men have more say in domestic affairs than women. When someone dies, most of the decision making is done by men. If the husband dies, some families ignore the rights of the wife and do all they can to dispossess her of her property. Although the pastor should not appear to be an arbiter in the distribution of inheritances among families, it is still the preacher's responsibility to advise through the gospel the best way for each member of the family to behave. Every situation is unique but an alert preacher will find opportunities in preaching at funerals to share, guide, counsel, admonish, encourage, empower, and in the end glorify the name of Jesus Christ, the risen Lord.

Chapter 3

How Do You Preach? A Repertoire of Skills

How to preach does not preclude what to preach. How to preach involves delivery as well as preparation and the message. Every step a preacher takes will finally add to how he or she preaches. For the purpose of streamlining discussion the how of preaching for this chapter will deal with what we preach from the pulpit and how it is communicated.

It is important that the techniques we use to communicate the gospel are biblically and culturally sound. Preaching is immersed in the discipline of communication, so the preacher must understand basic communication skills. As in any process of communication the goal is to be understood. In matters of the Christian faith the end does not necessarily justify the means. The manner and process through which the end has been attained must be equally justifiable. The use of any means of communication should not be an end in itself but be based on a sound theological explanation. Means of communicating the gospel should not be outside the shared cultural norms. Any experimental approach should be evaluated within the acceptable biblical, theological, and cultural boundaries.

A preacher's ability to deliver the gospel couched in all sorts of modes and models of communication is no substitute for a well thought-out and meaningful message. "It is never enough to know how to talk unless the speaker has something to say," noted R. E. C. Browne, "but he must never abandon the study of technique, for the man who neglects the science of his profession is soon at the end of his resources."[1] Browne went on to say, "The preacher's power to communicate depends upon his ability to interpret the pain of being human."[2] The method and content of preaching are in the last analysis inseparable. They complement each other. When issues on the cutting edge of life and experience form the message, the ways and means of communication are equally and naturally lively. More often than not, when the audience expresses disapproval of the speaker it is not because of the means of communication but because of what might have been said. The point of this discussion is to alert the reader that ways and means of communicating the gospel presented in this chapter should not be separated from the message. In preaching, the method of communication is an important aspect of the message.

This chapter will deal with techniques that enhance preaching, especially in the African context. In some cases an application of the discussed skill will be made to demonstrate possibilities for use by the preacher. The assumption is that there is no one method of communicating the gospel. What is important is that the preacher be aware of the existing clusters of skills in preaching from which to draw.

Use of Inclusive Language

The use of inclusive language may not seem that crucial for the preacher. While talk of the need for inclusive language in worship and in other areas of communication has taken root in the West, this is not yet so in Africa if we use Zimbabwe as an example.[3] Africa still is a patriarchal society whose women are marginalized. It is common to hear illustrations in sermons where a woman is the villain even when it is evident that a man was an accomplice. Gender sensitivity should be apparent in the African pulpit of today. The women in church are the same who hold meetings and attend symposia and workshops across the continent on gender issues. It is understandable when they assess the extent to which preachers recognize their presence. To be honest, if one wants to preach a harangue, it should be directed to the men of Africa rather than the women.

On one occasion a young woman preached at a section prayer meeting. She gave an illustration in which a woman had suffered at the hands of her husband. Interestingly, she apologized, saying she did not know who causes domestic problems but that the women are the ones who say enough is enough. The preacher was sensitive to the male-dominated society and hence she tried to be accommodating even though she was firm in concluding that women are on the receiving end of domestic violence. Rarely would you hear a male preacher saying clearly that women suffer at the hands of men. I am not saying that men don't preach sermons that depict the plight of women. But what is still needed is a more intentional inclusion of gender issues.

Another preacher started his sermon by rearranging the way the congregation sat. He wanted couples to sit together. The preacher was oblivious of single parents, widows and widowers, as well as the unmarried who were there. I remember well how those with no marriage partners exchanged glances that seemed to ask, "Are we wanted here?" Despite how the preacher developed the sermon, those people felt excluded, to the detriment of the overall impact of the preacher and his message.

Not only what the preacher says, but the whole mood and presentation of the sermon should be inviting to all in the congregation. Preaching must aim at drawing in all the people rather than excluding them. It is helpful to intentionally preach sermons that embrace all segments of the congregation. The preacher should make use of research in the discipline of psychology on the emotional needs of different age groups. The youth need to hear their issues occasionally raised in the pulpit, as do the elderly.

The African preacher has a significant role to play in the use of inclusive language. It isn't necessary to tell the congregation that we are on a crusade of fostering inclusive language. Sometimes we are more effective when people learn from the way we behave and speak than when we merely express our intention.

Use of Proverbs

One of the signs that an African is conversant in an indigenous language is an occasional foray into the proverbs. The use of proverbs transforms language analogically from a liquid state into a solid entity. By using proverbs the preacher indirectly announces to the congregation that he or she is in touch with the repository of traditional wisdom and is therefore contextual. The people show appreciation when hearing such a refined form of expression.

On Easter Sunday, 23 April 2000, I preached a sermon at St. Peter's United Church Methodist, Mutare, Zimbabwe, in English for the benefit of international members. My translator, Mr. Chris Makufa, did a marvelous job. In the sermon I emphasized that whether one finds him or herself depressed or having it all, the Resurrection of Jesus Christ is the greatest experience offered to everyone who believes. In the translation, Mr. Makufa used a Shona proverb, saying the Resurrection of Jesus Christ is even for those "*Vanoti kutakura mutoro mbudzi ihata.*" Meaning the Resurrection of Jesus Christ is important in every situation, even for those who are so rich that when they want to carry something they use a goat directly on their heads to relieve the pressure. I am aware that outside the African culture where people still carry loads on their heads, the proverb may lose its punch. But for that African congregation in Mutare on that Easter Sunday, the proverb brought the world of the rich before them in vivid terms. No wonder there was spontaneous applause and laughter in response to the expression—something they had not done in response to my English expression of the same sentiments.

The use of proverbs in African culture is so prevalent that even African journalists resort to them to make a point in their reports in the media. Referring to the political situation in Zimbabwe, a reporter used an Igbo proverb in one of the Zimbabwe independent newspapers. The proverb says, "A man who brings a maggot-infested rag into his house should not be shocked when ants start visiting him."[4] It means that when you do something bad, don't be surprised when you suffer the consequences. In the same paper, another proverb appeared in Shona saying, "*Dindiringwe rinonaka richakweva rimwe, kana rave iro roti mavara azara ivhu*" (People are happy when they have everything going their way, and quickly cry foul when someone else starts benefiting).[5] These proverbs summarized the issues in a way that long, detailed articles could not. Although other cultures use proverbs, the aural nature of communication among Africans highlights their use. Mercy Amba Oduyoye noted that the popularity of proverbs among Africans is vouchsafed by their continued use and through the concerted efforts of Africans to gather and put them into writing.[6]

African authors have long acknowledged the role of proverbs in the African culture in general and in African preaching in particular. The significance of proverbs lies in their role in forming "a mnemonic device in societies in which everything worth knowing and relevant to day-to-day life has to be committed to memory."[7] The Yoruba people of Nigeria have captured the importance of proverbs in their culture by saying, "Proverbs are horses we ride to search for truth."[8] Again from Nigerian culture, "Proverbs are the palm oil with which words are eaten."[9] In addition, there is a communal ownership of the wisdom enriched by proverbs. Thus Alex J. C. Pongweni could write, "Proverbs, metaphors, similes and idiophones are generally not for the artist to create or coin *ex vacuo*. They derive from, and express the communal view of the world based on first hand experience. As such they simultaneously belong to each and everyone."[10]

Kurewa reminded the African preacher of the role that idioms and proverbs play in African speech making.[11] Other authors pointed out that preachers and teachers in Shona culture are fond of using proverbs.[12] However, encouraging African preachers to use proverbs without an examination of their multifaceted nature might lead to some communication "hiccups" in the delivery of sermons. An example that comes to mind is a Shona proverb, "*Mbudzi kudya mufenje kutodza mai.*"

The proverb translates "For a goat to eat leaves of a mufenje tree is to be like its mother."

Let us imagine that one is preaching a sermon urging people to be perfect as their God is in heaven. On the surface it appears appropriate to say, "In our Shona language we have a proverb, "*mbudzi kudya mufenje kutodza mai*" (Therefore we are called upon to be like our God in heaven). Such application will create problems in the minds of the hearers. First, the proverb is usually used by male chauvinists when children are misbehaving. The point is that their mischief is derived from the mother. Such type of illogical conclusion thrived in a society that marginalized women. Second, no matter how much we try to be perfect we cannot imitate God. Thus, to use such a proverb will create some communication blocks especially among women hearers. Therefore a look at the nature of proverbs is necessary before we urge preachers to use them.

Most of the writers on this subject focused on the positive role of proverbs without assessing problematic uses as we already illustrated. For one, the meaning of proverbs might change with the passage of time.[13] A preacher may use a proverb whose intended meaning is no longer the one evoked in the minds of the hearers. Because proverbs are a form of refined speech par excellence, it follows that not everyone in a community can be expected to understand them. An interesting but equally problematic form of protocols for the preacher is that in Shona culture the young do not quote proverbs to their elders. On this point Pongweni has this to say:

> The proverb is marked not only by its fixed work-order, but the tone of voice, explicit or implied, is also an integral part. And this tone of voice imbues the proverb utterance with a sense of authority and impersonality. This impersonality and ex-cathedra quality of proverb utterance probably explains why, at least in Shona culture, the young dare not quote proverbs to their elders.[14]

The notion that older age denotes wisdom is a commonly held view among Africans. I once asked some students at Africa University in Zimbabwe about the relationship of age and the attainment of wisdom in African culture. Those from Angola, Mozambique, and Zimbabwe in my Christian Education class of 1994 agreed that the elders were regarded as the repositories of wisdom. How then does a young preacher use proverbs in a congregation where elders are present? This is indeed a problem, even though the office of the pastor is highly regarded among Africans of all ages. However, the young preacher should use proverbs in a way that exudes familiarity and adequate knowledge of their meaning. If elders conclude that the pastor is misusing the proverbs, he or she loses respect not because of age but ignorance.

Another issue related to the use of proverbs in preaching in African context is that new ones are formed and continually find their way in the common vocabulary of the people. This rise of new proverbs is prevalent in urban centers where the young are detached from the elders.[15] An example of a new proverb in Shona language could be: "*Muchena kubata paindihanzi ndava mbozhawo.*" This literally translates, "A poor man holding a pint of beer thinks he is rich too."[16] Traditionally, African beer was not commercialized. But now that those in cities show their conspicuous consumption through the purchase of beer, a new proverb has emerged. The preacher can always check the authenticity of these proverbs by consulting with elders.

Further, some of these wisdom sayings are misogynous. "Why should women not feel free to dismantle those proverbs that are sexist, oppressive or limiting to the full growth of their humanity and the just ordering of society?" asked Oduyoye.[17] Most if not all African societies have proverbs that portray women as appendages of men. For instance, in the Nigerian culture there are such proverbs as: "Women love where wealth is," and "While the male soul is alive, the female soul does not crack nuts."[18] There is this one from the Tonga of Zambia, "He who listens to women suffered from famine at harvest time."[19]

Of interest is Bourdillon's analysis that in themselves proverbs do not tell us much about the world. They are used to affirm the speaker's opinion by referring to traditional wisdom. Bourdillon took note of Bloch's observation that proverbs and other similar forms of speech are ritualistic in nature. Like all rituals, such forms of speech serve to confirm those in positions of leadership in the community.[20] All these examples discussed so far should serve as a reminder to the African preacher to be selective in the use of proverbs.

Let us illustrate how a preacher might use proverbs in a sermon. In Shona culture there is a proverb that says, "*Chawaona idya nehama mutorwa ane hanganwa*." It means when you get something to eat, share it with relatives because a stranger will forget. Such a proverb could be used in a homily for a Holy Communion service. The preacher can point out that Jesus Christ regarded the disciples as his relatives and decided to eat the Last Supper with them. To this day Christians come to the communion table not as strangers but as close relatives of our Lord and Savior Jesus Christ.

Although not writing about the use of proverbs in preaching, Choan-Seng Song echoed this approach of relating the Eucharist to Asian cultural motifs. He relates how an Asian mother remembered her son who had died in war by ritually filling "her son's bowl with fresh rice every day."[21] The bowl of rice became a symbol of hope and a uniting force between the living and the dead. Song concluded his study by pointing out that Asians will find in the Lord's Supper "the promise and reality of life they are seeking through the bowl of rice."[22] A people's culture can provide a legitimate entry into the mysteries of the events of salvation.

Other proverbs can be related to different events and stories in the Bible. What comes to mind is a sermon based on the story of Joseph and his brothers. The incident where Potiphar's wife attempted to lure and force Joseph to sleep with her is conducive to a Shona proverbial application. The proverb says, "*Nhamo inhamo zvayo mai haaroodzwi*." This means that no matter how much pain and suffering one might experience, there will be no thought of giving away one's mother in marriage. In African marriages there is payment of *lobola*. The implication is that you cannot expect to solve your financial problems by giving away your mother in marriage. Joseph was determined to resist. He concluded that in spite of the impending pain and banishment from his master's household, he was not going to give away his mother in marriage. The preacher could go on to explain that this determination to resist temptation at all cost is what God expects of us. Application of proverbs to sermons calls upon the resourcefulness of each individual preacher.

Imagination in Preaching

Upon reading emerging literature in homiletics from the West one is confronted with the concept of imagination in preaching. The angle taken is that imagination is a skill that can be taught to preachers.[23] One wonders whether there has been a time when preaching was possible without imagination. Imagination is an integral part of preaching from jotting random notes in a notebook, to exegesis, and finally, delivery. It is misleading to suggest imagination is an option for the preacher. When Jesus Christ taught that the Kingdom of God is like this or that, he used imagination to express the way things are and also called upon the hearers to imagine with him. Preaching always involves imagination.

In preaching there is a process of incarnating the sermon by making the preached word assume an identifiable life of its own within the experiences of the listeners. My biblical text for understanding imagination is 1 John 1:1: "That which was from the beginning, which we have heard, which we have seen with our eyes, which we have looked upon and touched with our hands, concerning the word of life . . ." Preaching with imagination aims at helping people hear the risen Jesus Christ, and see and touch him through the sermon. In the words of Urban J. Holmes III, imagination is "that capacity in man to make the material an image of the immaterial or spiritual."[24] Or as Barbara Brown Taylor put it: "For preachers imagination is the ability to form images in the minds of their listeners that are not physically present to their senses, so that they find themselves in a wider world with new choices about who and how they will be."[25]

The African worldview is still amenable to creative imagination. Determinant factors that shape the African's mindset are not wholly based on a scientific worldview. Africans readily accept without question beliefs and assertions irrespective of whether they stand or fall under scientific scrutiny.[26] In comparing the oral African culture and the ocular Western culture, Edward P. Wimberly pointed out that the Western culture focuses on what can be seen, and is based on reason and logic. He wrote that Western culture "prizes the rational, logical, abstract, and intellectual dimensions of religious expression more than the emotive, celebrative, poetic, communal, relational, and storytelling and story listening dimensions so strongly characteristic of oral culture."[27]

The Western world approaches imagination with suspicion and attempts to make sense out of it by imposing a framework through which imaginative faculties could be cultivated and taught. By suggesting that preachers need lessons in how to imagine through their sermon, the process of imagination is stultified. Imagination thrives naturally in a culture freed from the endless demands to prove oneself, even in matters of faith.

I remember my first experience in a systematic theology class in which our Western professor confidently announced that the lesson for the day was to provide proof for the existence of God. We students exchanged glances of disbelief. How do you prove the existence of God by means of external references to mountains, rivers, and other matter, if you do not have the inner feeling to vouchsafe for the existence of a creator? For the African, belief in God becomes a reality as a result of one's imagination, which should be given free rein. The African environment and worldview encourages sensitivity to imagination.

For preaching, imagination must be viewed as imagistic presentation of the biblical message. By imagistic presentation I mean imagination and resourcefulness in the presentation of the gospel. For me the process should not be different from a newspaper article advising people to be imaginative with their salads. "Use your imagination with your salads," wrote one author. "Make them more into a meal on their own, attractively presented . . . then people will eat them and compliment the cook."[28] An imaginative sermon is a meal to the soul of the listener and is edible. Scott Paul Wilson describes the imagination of the heart "as the bringing together of two ideas that might not otherwise be connected and developing the creative energy they generate."[29] This is fine, but imagination is not confined to ideas and concepts but embraces the whole spectrum of being, and hence imagistic presentation with focus on tangible images.

In order to clarify imagistic presentation of the gospel let us go through some illustrative material. While I was serving as pastor at Old Mutare Mission in Zimbabwe, we invited a guest preacher for Easter. In one of his sermons Reverend Thomas Muhomba brought to the church a beautiful basket. We waited expectantly to see what was in that container. When the preacher opened the basket, to our surprise we were shown a dead snake! Muhomba's point was that people present a false image of themselves, and yet inwardly they have rotten characters like that dead snake. This approach may shock someone from another culture. But for an African preacher presenting the message contextually going to such an extent is memorable and acceptable to the hearer.

In another sermon on the Rich Fool, a preacher began by telling the congregation that he wanted to paint a portrait of a farmer and his surroundings.[30] He went on to say that the rich farmer had a house near a mountain on the farm. There were lots of cattle, sheep, and chickens. In the fields one could see horses and people working in the gardens. Everything was green on the farm, and the farmer did well as a result of hard work. As the preacher talked, he imitated an artist painting. All the time he focused on one corner as if an actual portrait was being painted. Finally the preacher asked, "Why would Jesus Christ call him a fool and yet he is a model of hard work?" The sermon then unfolded as he explained the foolishness of this man.

This is an example of imagistic presentation where the process of imagination focuses on the creation of images. The preacher was immersed in the process with both mind and body. As he looked at the imaginary picture the congregation likewise saw their own farms. In the case of our preacher the observable environment fed into his imaginative mind. The farmer's description fits the African white commercial farmers who usually build their mansions near mountains on the farm. Horses and many cattle are part of the scene at a commercial farm. The listeners could not miss the context. Imagistic presentation in a sermon gets inspiration from ordinary life situations. It moves from the abstract to the concrete.

The Language of Preaching

The language of preaching includes every aspect of skill expressed through spoken words. But we still need to speak about language of preaching as a skill on its own. The main feature about language of preaching is that it must be concrete. I am reminded of a young boy who prayed for everyone in the room. As if to make sure that God knew the people, the boy called each name then walked to where the person was and touched him or her. The language of preaching is not simply words, but words that make the hearer also see, touch, feel, and smell. The preacher uses words that are evocative in nature, that turn ideas into action. For example, *love* is sitting down with your children and giving them your valuable time. *Justice* is transformed into standing for the rights of others even when none of your own rights have been violated. As Barbara Brown Taylor said, preach using language that "appeals to the eye, the nose, the tongue and the skin as well as to the ear. It has weight and scent to it, texture and temperature."[31] Our ears receive the spoken word for the purpose of distributing it to other senses. When the listener hears the preached word, it should immediately activate visual receptors, taste buds, tactual, and other senses. When Jesus Christ described his followers as "the salt of the earth," he used concrete language that evoked sensory responses in the hearer. There are numerous examples in the Bible of language of the concrete and the sensed.

For Colin Morris the language of preaching should be economical, that is, use few words but be to the point. Further, the preacher should use euphony, words that are easily linked without effort. Finally the preacher must focus on sensuousness, words that play on the five senses.[32] There is a Shona idiom that says, "N*yoka iripo haiwedzi negayi.*" This translates, "A snake that is there cannot be measured by means of bark fibre." The meaning is that you should not waste time explaining something when people can see for themselves or can hear firsthand from the person involved. That is what preached words should do—take the people to where the action is.

As observed in the Shona culture in Zimbabwe, pictorial language is characteristic of African conversation. When asked how old a child back home is, the traditional response is not to give their age in years. Instead, one raises the hand to the estimated height of the child, even though the question was not how tall. Africans act out the spoken word whenever and wherever possible. A men's group, the *wabvuwi* or fishermen, in The United Methodist Church, videotaped a song: "U*penyu hwangu nemasimba*" ("My life and energy or power"). The hymn has a stanza that talks about waiting for the Lord. In the video the singers actually sit down to demonstrate the action in the words. For Africans, performing the spoken word is expected and accepted.

One Easter I was paired with a woman guest preacher whose sermon about Mary, the mother of Jesus, witnessing and reacting to the Crucifixion is still vivid in my mind. She brought a huge cross in the church and wailed under it as Mary did. Not only that, but she also went down on the floor and wriggled in pain as if imitating Mary. A careful study of the circumstances then does not confirm the way the woman preacher performed the spoken word. But that is beside the point, which was to verbalize the pain Mary suffered and to demonstrate it for all to see.

"Some of the most vivid and arresting metaphors appear in the sermons of unlettered black preachers," observed Lischer.[33] Those in the West believe that everything worthwhile must be formally taught. The African-American preachers to which Lischer referred were uneducated or unlettered in other ways but did not fail to draw from the residual African heritage that has remained part of them. Even in Africa one does not go through educational litany in order to become effective in the use of metaphor. An oral culture encircles its spoken languages with images, hence the saturation with metaphor.

Languages of preaching should be variably informed by one's culture and experiences of the people. The preacher should be conversant with formal and informal expressions of different subgroups in a culture. Know what the youth are saying and seeing on TV, and use that language when possible in preaching the gospel. There was a drama on Zimbabwe television with a character who used the slang *biggers* to mean big, superior, and all powerful. During the days when the drama was shown, I preached a sermon in which I said that there is no *biggers* whatsoever above Jesus Christ. The response was overwhelming from both the youth and the adults. Every preacher should have the ability to hold the attention of the congregation; it is a crucial step in the sermon positively impacting the lives of the people. The Christian faith must be "incarnated in and enriched by the local mentality, language, culture, and aspirations of the people."[34] An effective preacher would leave no stone unturned in search of cultural motifs to graft onto the sermon. Opportunities abound but we need to be conscious and intentional in exercising the skill.

I am a regular guest preacher at Holy Name Anglican Church in Sakubva, Mutare, Zimbabwe. On one occasion I was invited to preach on giving to God. In the sermon I said that some people give to God an amount of money equal to what is given for *gupuro*. *Gupuro* is money given by a husband to the wife indicating that the marriage has hit the rocks and she must return to her parents. This custom among the Shona has a stipulated fee of twenty-five cents or some other small amount. In preparing the sermon little did I imagine that the term *gupuro* was to dominate all other ideas I had planned to share. There were positive echoes in their prayers and verbal feedback to me after the sermon. They interpreted rightly that giving stingily to God is like divorcing him. This word has been in the Shona vocabulary from time immemorial but the people heard it in a new way that day.

Preaching as Storytelling

According to Ian Pitt-Watson, proclaiming the gospel is "an oral, aural event."[35] Maybe nowhere has the power of the story been captured better than by Henry H. Mitchell:

> Perhaps it is too painful to concede the superiority of "primitive" folk culture's encouchment of the most profound wisdom in tales . . . The superiority of tales and the like lies in the fact that people "see" the issue more clearly in pictures and plots. Indeed, they not only grasp ideas better: they also encounter them with their whole personhood, because they identify with the details and personalities and their activities.[36]

For the African preacher, storytelling is the normative approach to effective communication of the gospel. Africans traditionally explain events through creative stories. I remember being told a story that explained the origins of a nearby valley in the vicinity of our village. The story is that two mountains fought and the defeated one ran away. In the process of running away a valley was formed behind it. In African culture, we are seldom given yes-or-no answers to questions, but are answered with a story or extended conversation.

Homileticians in the West have recently discovered the value of storytelling. What the West has done is to name what Africans have been doing ever since time began. Westerners are revolting against the three-point argumentative approach to preaching. They have discovered that the Bible is a book of stories.[37] What is forgotten is not only that the Bible has stories and therefore calls for preaching based on stories but also that the church as a community of believers should tell their stories. People are full of stories that constitute their lives. Some of these stories are joyous, while some are sorrowful. People come to church not to hear arguments to score points but to hear the origin of all stories. When the African sings, "Tell me the stories of Jesus," that rings a concordant message in the mind of the African hearer. African children grow up demanding to be told stories by the elders. The church as a community does not thrive on arguments but on a friendly discourse. Anyone familiar with storytelling realizes that argumentative discussion immediately falls away when a story is told. By its very nature the church as a community is an extension of the village. Stories bring and keep villages together.

As already alluded to, African children grow up in an environment that cultivates storytelling as they listen to fables almost every evening. Grandmothers and grandfathers usually are entrusted with the task of telling these fables. My father was so effective in telling these fables that sometimes I could find myself standing close to the door fearing that the animal he was describing was about to get me. Not only is listening involved, but also the child is involved in learning the art of storytelling. As I look back I have come to realize that these fables were not only told for entertainment but also as a way of training the children in how to tell stories. In the Zimbabwean system of education there is time set aside for children to tell stories. A magazine carried a report about the Chimanimani musical group on tour in

England where they conducted musical shows and lessons in "African dancing, African drumming, storytelling, and singing at schools and recreational centres."[38]

Storytelling is not usually consciously taught in African stories. The teaching happens in subtle ways rather than through planned analytical structure of what constitutes a story and how to tell stories. In Africa, stories are lived experiences of the people because they dream about them, they observe those who tell them, and quickly exchange roles and become participants in telling their own stories rather than remain as observers. Teaching stories where communal life has disintegrated becomes a superficial exercise. Stories belong to communities of people, not to individuals.

Storytelling is not so much a preaching skill as an integral part of the message. Like any other skill or technique in preaching, the story is meaningful if it serves to enhance the whole. There are many ways of storytelling in a sermon. One could tell a story in the form of an illustration, as is true for the parables of Jesus Christ. The other approach is re-telling the biblical story adding height, depth, feelings, and mannerisms to the characters. Re-telling the story demands that the story be transported from ancient Palestine to my round hut where the listeners are seated in a semicircle. The narrative gets encapsulated in the existing cultural motifs. As the story develops the hearer is discretely asked to pay attention to some moral teaching as it relates to his/her daily experiences. Below is one example of storytelling based again on the story of Joseph, one that includes a sermon segment at the beginning.

Some still vividly remember the drought that ravaged Zimbabwe in 1992. The government made available some farms where people could take their livestock for grazing. People left their homes and families and went to far away areas of the country where they had never been before. The Bible tells us that Jacob's sons herded sheep far away from home, not because of a drought but because rich grazing areas were no longer available near home. From time to time provision was sent to them. Most of us can still remember when food had to be brought to where we were working in the fields because there was no time to go back home. Sometimes when we are involved in busy and life-saving situations there is no time to go home to eat. Have you ever experienced a situation in which going back home to eat is a waste of time? This was the condition in which Jacob's sons found themselves.

We encounter Joseph as he is taking provisions to the brothers. Unknown to the father and to the innocent young Joseph, intense jealousy gripped the hearts and minds of the brothers. Jealousy can create a chasm between people of the same family. More often than not, our chief's court meets to settle family feuds in this village. Sons and daughters of the same family fight over allocation of garden plots or over the ownership of cattle. Likewise, Jacob's elder sons were so estranged from their young brother that they could not even call him by his own name. All they could utter was "there comes a dreamer!" When hatred reigns, people call each other names.

The story could go on with vivid images unfolding in the description. Storytelling is applied to the biblical story by interweaving it with the lived experience of the hearers. In this case feuds among family members links the story of the Bible with the people. Interweaving the story of the text and real-life situations readily opens preaching up to contextualization. Be aware, though, of the temptation to tell stories as an art and to make them an end to themselves without any meaningful connection with the biblical text.

Use of Song

Africans are singing people. All people sing, but for Africans singing is spontaneous and is part of most events and daily activities. There are songs for working in the fields, songs for milking cows, and so forth. Through singing, messages are communicated from one person to another. My father's brother used to sing a song whose meaning I could not understand when I was young. He would sing, "M*ombe dzababa dzakapera nemakiwa*." I don't remember the rest because he repeated more of this one than the others. The stanza says, "My father's cattle were finished by white people." I now know that he was singing of the experiences of property deprivation that Africans suffered under colonial occupation, especially during the early encounters between Africans and Europeans. Listening to the piece of music was not all that palatable but as Francis Bebey wrote: "African musicians do not seek to combine sounds in a manner pleasing to the ear. Their aim is simply to express life in all of its aspects through the medium of sound."[39]

"In line with African tradition, special songs are composed for particular occasions or to honour individuals," observed H. W. Turner, "and there is no hesitation about singing these in worship."[40] An African preacher is expected to embellish the sermon with songs. As Ndiokwere noted, "Even in the pulpit the homeliest is sure to win sympathy, attention and admiration of the congregation when he intersperses his homily with short songs . . ."[41] From the preaching events I have witnessed in Zimbabwe I have observed that for those who can do it, interweaving the sermon with singing is an experience the congregation never tires of. Turner also noted, "The preaching may last five minutes or two hours . . . , relieved by choruses at intervals, and there is close attention, with amens and other exclamation of agreement."[42]

Although Turner referred to a report on the worship practices of African independent churches, what happens in those churches concerning singing during the sermon holds for the mainline Protestant churches in Africa as well. The *mvet* players and storytellers of Cameroon intersperse their stories with songs.

> The laughter that interrupts the story at this point corresponds to the falling of the curtain at the end of an act. The audience, which has been listening intently up to this point, relaxes for a few moments while the *mvet* player asks, "What can your ears hear?" and the crowd shouts back, "They can hear the *mvet*." So the *mvet* strikes up, sometimes solo and sometimes to accompany a song in which the entire audience participates.[43]

So for African preachers, singing as part of the sermon is integral to their traditional culture.

Interestingly, it is not always the preacher who initiates the singing. Anyone in the congregation may start a song during the sermon. In fact the preacher may see this as a complimentary response to the sermon. In the interest of order and organization during worship service, something that the missionaries taught, few people are willing to start a song from within the congregation unless the preacher asks for it.

These characteristics of African worship have roots in traditional cultures and must not be allowed to die. Africans are spontaneous in a number of activities, more so in singing where everyone joins in with total disregard of required expertise. It is this spontaneity that the African church has stifled in an attempt to keep worship orderly. To be true to its heritage, the African church and the preacher in particular must deliberately encourage these traits.

Sometimes the preacher breaks into song at the start of the sermon to activate the congregation. In some cases the song comes at intervals during the sermon. Some preachers stick to one song that serves as a refrain throughout the sermon. The usual practice is to sing more than one song along the way. Other preachers give a brief introduction to explain how they perceive the song and the story of the text. Let us imagine that the preacher has talked about the suffering and imprisonment of St. Paul. Our preacher could then put a song into St. Paul's mouth: "*Jehova Mufidzi wangu handichazoshayiwa ndiye anondiradzika pane mafuro ake,*" a Shona translation of Psalm 23. The preacher would then explain that St. Paul sang the song fully trusting his life in the hands of God, the Shepherd.

As we know, exegesis will fall apart if we try to find when and where St. Paul sang such a song. But it is such liberty to imagine and express feelings that make African preaching not only enlivening to the text but also lively for the listeners. After all, the Apostles sang in prison, so what is wrong in giving them a song the people could identify with and join in singing?

Another example of the use of song in preaching happened in a sermon by Reverend Tsaurai Mapfeka, a graduate student at Africa University, as he preached at St. Peter's United Methodist, Inner City, Mutare, Zimbabwe on 2 April 2000. He took his song not from the hymnbook but from the gospel singers who appear on national television. In Shona the song says, "*Waigara zvakanaka nevamwe muraini*," adding and repeating these words that mean, "The person lived well with others in the neighbourhood." It is a song usually sung at funerals giving positive testimony about the deceased's life.

Mapfeka was preaching on the events of the Crucifixion of Jesus Christ. His point was that because of mob psychology some people who were helped by Jesus Christ wished him dead, simply to remain acceptable to the crowd and to their neighbours. We do things sometimes to meet the social contracts we have in our communities and not for the good cause. Together with the congregation he sang the short song at intervals in the sermon. More interesting, he cautioned the congregation not to raise their voices too much because, as he said, "We are at a funeral." When people's experiences are raised in the sermon to be confronted with the word of the biblical text, preaching becomes a meaningful conversation.

Illustrations

Obviously, Fred Craddock is right to a great extent when he says that if careful attention is given to the language of the sermon there is no need for illustrations.[44] The new homiletic should no longer rely on illustrations to clarify points in the sermon. What needs emphasis is the use of concrete language that appeals not only to the ear but to multiple senses. Too much focus on illustrations is an admission that sermon content is weak and the ideas intelligible. When we engage in normal conversation about the journey we have undertaken we don't rely on illustrations to clarify our experiences. Instead, we describe those encounters as clearly as possible.

Nevertheless, I have carefully said Craddock is right to a great extent because I strongly believe that illustrations in the form of realistic and meaningful stories are necessary especially in the African pulpit. As already noted, the African communal life is still based on storytelling. The African hearer of the sermon is still attuned to storytelling and likes to hear stories in a sermon. I would not go the whole way with Craddock in saying there is no need for illustrations, irrespective of how the sermon is based on concrete speech forms.

Illustrations play other essential roles in sermons. I am thinking of the psychological dimension in which illustrations help the congregation to rest. We who have listened attentively to a sermon can remember times when we felt whipped up emotionally and wished for the preacher to do something to cool us down. An illustration, when appropriately introduced into the sermon, has the effect of relaxing the hearer and prepares him or her to move on with the preacher. Preachers who churn out a series of ideas with no intermittent stories usually tread the path of failure, irrespective of how forcefully such thoughts are explained.

On the other side of this is when African preachers string stories together like beads of different colours. In such cases the stories come one after another without any substantial ideas pulling them toward a certain focus. Illustrations are not appendages to the theme of the sermon but are an integral part of the content. Still, they need to be attached to some coherent ideas. It is a mark of a weak sermon if people remember a story but fail to recall what the preacher was communicating by that illustration.

I once sent students to do field research for a worship project. In my naïve approach as a junior instructor, I read as much as possible from available literature on worship. As the authors said, I also became convinced that worship must be interesting.[45] So I prepared a questionnaire for the students to use in their interviews with pastors in and around Mutare. One of the questions asked pastors what they did to make worship interesting. When a Roman Catholic student asked a Catholic priest this question, she was clearly told that the purpose of worship is not to interest people.

That response made me revisit my agreement with those authors who say that worship should be interesting. Homileticians write as a matter of fact that illustrations make sermons interesting.[46] The problem lies in the fact that the context in which *interesting* is used is not usually clarified. If by *interesting* we merely mean to excite people's feelings and attitudes to warm up to the preacher, then that is not what worship and preaching in particular is meant to be. For illustrations to be of interest in the sermon, they need to draw the attention of the hearer to that which is essential by blocking off other competing attractions and detractors. In that case we can subscribe to the idea that illustrations make sermons interesting.

Related to this issue of making the sermon interesting is the idea that illustrations help make the sermon memorable. We must redefine the meaning of memory when related to a sermon. When hearers remember sermons as demonstrated through sharing with those who might not have heard that particular sermon, that is lower level memory. But when an illustration helps the listener to commit to memory the whole sermon or larger chunks of it and that memory is transformed into behavioral and attitudinal changes, that is higher level memory. In other words, illustrations should be remembered through action and not only cognitively.

Buttrick has stipulated some criteria for an illustration that are worth sharing. First, the analogical relationships between the illustration and the idea to be clarified must be clear. Second, the nature of the sermon content and the form or structure of the illustration should be agreeable. Third, illustrations should readily blend and measure up to the content of the sermon.[47] In addition, Spain has other helpful points regarding criteria for illustrations: Illustrations should be in good taste, those related to personal family affairs should be used sparingly, and must suit the particular congregation.[48] Avoid illustrations that give the outward impression that they are suitable for use in any sermon. Also avoid illustrations that need explanation.

Where do we find illustrations? While there are books of illustrations, it is a blessing in disguise that African preachers do not have those resources readily accessible. There is a mortifying effect on the sermon when illustrations are removed from the immediate human experience of the congregation. Illustrations should be alive in themselves before they enliven the sermon because they are true to the lives of this particular congregation at this point in time. Like sermon ideas come from people's ordinary life experiences, illustrations should come from the same source too.

The preacher's wide reading, travel, the Bible, and borrowing from others are all sources for illustrations. We should be cautious not to use those illustrations merely to show how widely read we are. The criteria referred to above must guide the preacher. Illustrations from the Bible are applicable for all times and a preacher will do well to use them. However, listening to sermons by my students in which illustrations are taken from biblical stories, I have noticed that they overshadow everything said in that sermon. The reason is obvious—these are biblical texts that beg to be preached on their own. They refuse to be bushes but become forests in the sermon.

I have developed the following guidelines for using stories from the Bible as illustrations. First, make sure that the story is well known by almost everyone in that congregation. Second, avoid retelling the whole story and instead make reference to it, touching on the key aspects to refresh the people's memory. Third, assert whether what happened in that biblical story is common experience for the listeners to the extent each and every one could identify with the story. We cannot, for instance, use Saul's conversion on the road to Damascus in the sense that God expects everyone who believes to have an exact experience. But the preacher can legitimately use that story to call upon individuals to recall their own experience of how they encountered the presence of Jesus Christ and the Holy Spirit in their lives. Fourth, use biblical illustrations sparingly and avoid being addicted to them. Anything lifted from the Bible is not necessarily good for the sermon. Illustrations require careful selection.

Another point is that illustrations offer the greatest opportunity for the contextualization of the gospel. The African preacher should search for illustrations from among typical African stories. I have noticed (and I do that intentionally) that each time I say "in our African context" people show overt signs of paying attention. The elders seem be saying, *Tell us so that we can learn about our heritage.* So the preacher is given an open cheque to fill with whatever amount of content from the African experience.

It is no wonder that Jesus Christ chose to say, "A sower went out to sow . . ." when it was probable that the listeners actually saw a sower across the stream in the fields. We shouldn't scratch our heads in search of illustrations; instead we should scratch our people's past and experiences. The best illustrations are those to which the people can relate and acknowledge to themselves that the experience happened to them or to someone they know. When we use illustrations removed from the immediate context of the congregation, we need to restructure the content of the illustration using language familiar to the listeners. This means that in African context we use idioms and proverbs and other forms of speech and Africanize that story from whatever part of the world it might have originated. For example, if the incident for our illustration happened near a river below a mountain, we give familiar names to that river and mountain.

After all, what is preaching if it is not naming that which the hearers already know? "It is out of our spiritual perception of life that the deepest illustrations will come for our preaching because they are at best part of natural theology," said Donald English.[49] One might add that "spiritual perception of life" is made possible through the preacher's intermingling with other people in pastoral and other arenas.

Introduction to the Sermon

The dominant method of introducing a sermon in African context is to introduce both the preacher and the sermon to create rapport. Introducing the preacher does not focus on academic credentials and other professional experience. What matters is that the introduction tells the congregation where the preacher is coming from spiritually. No other form of introducing the sermon will do the job for an African congregation. Whether the preacher is an invited guest or the regular pastor, it is important not to overlook this state of affairs type of introduction.

In 1976, I attended a church service in Bloomington, Indiana, USA, where the preacher was an African-American. He had experienced some problems with his eyes during the weekend. When he started the sermon he assured the congregation that although he was not seeing clearly, his spiritual eyes were as clear as ever before. I said to myself, *I am surely back on the African continent.* That approach of spiritualizing every experience and sharing with the congregation in the introduction of the sermon is a common feature in African preaching. In Shona culture introductions are so crucial that they become elaborate when an issue is to be discussed. Everyone within the family must be informed according to their ranks in the extended family. At any gathering new arrivals introduce their presence through clapping of hands joined by those already present and then everybody feels comfortable.

One other way in which African preachers introduce their sermons is by way of a song. The song may be one that calls upon the Holy Spirit to give the preacher what to say or any other song that affirms the messenger's beliefs. If a song is not used the preacher may call upon a member of the congregation to introduce (*kusuma*) the preacher to

God. This is always done in the form of a prayer. At times the congregation itself through the worship leader selects a song for the purpose of presenting (*kusvitsa*) the preacher to God. From my observation of what happens in the African churches in Zimbabwe, it is not the actual introduction of the sermon that matters but that of the preacher. The sermon introduction is a second phase following that of the preacher.

I urge African preachers not to abandon this two-prolonged type of introduction in the sermon. Having said that, we are still not aware of what the actual sermon introduction is meant to do and how it could be done. Preaching involves a battle of wits and the preacher must be prepared to win people's attention. Every sermon introduction must have an element of surprise that leads the people to want to hear what follows. I don't want to give the exaggerated notion that it is only the introduction of the sermon that should capture the attention of the congregation. My point of view is that every segment of the sermon must manage to call for the listener's attention. But this element of surprise will go a long way in the process of connecting the listener and the preacher.

If you begin a sermon on God's love by saying, "God loves you all," someone is bound to say, "So what?" Those who are polite may wonder why there is no inner flicker ignited by that statement. But if the same is said to some people in the remote corner of the world who have no idea that they are the objects of God's love, then that statement could attract their attention. So an introduction is determined by a host of factors characteristic of the congregation. For those familiar with the Christian faith the same sermon on God's love could be introduced by saying, "I am so surprised that God could decide to sacrifice his only Son, Jesus Christ, for creatures called human beings . . ." Here is an element of the unusual that contradicts the norm and listeners want to hear how the preacher will get out of the bind.

By their inherent nature stories have an element of surprise. The story should introduce the sermon, not display that the preacher is an artful storyteller. This story could be any or the one within the biblical text. Related to the story in the text is an explanation of the text as a way of introducing the sermon. This is the opportunity to share the few but relevant exegetical fruits with the congregation. Most listeners of sermons do not have an in-depth knowledge about how it was in the biblical world and are usually surprised when they hear. Again, the idea is not to show how learned we are.

Here are some rules of thumb to keep in mind about sermon introductions: 1) Vary your approach so that the congregation does not predict the way you will start, 2) Give adequate attention to the introduction when preparing the sermon, and 3) Remember that the introduction gives the congregation a chance to enter into a covenant with you that they will listen to what you have to say. Most homileticians agree that the purpose of the sermon introduction is "to help the congregation in the conversation of the sermon."[50] While it is important to understand different types of introductions and how to use them, it is even more urgent for the preacher to come to grips with the purpose of sermon introductions.

Conclusion of the Sermon

The best and most important conclusion to a sermon is not the one the preacher makes but what follows as a response from the congregation. If all sermons ended with the response that Peter and the other Apostles received from the people who heard them preach, "Brethren, what shall we do?" (Acts 2:37[b]), there would be nothing more to say about sermon conclusions. A lot is written about how to conclude sermons. The problem is that like introductions the focus is more on methods than on the purpose. Conclusions for sermons must be effective to the mental faculties. As one preacher put it, preaching aims at a verdict where the listener is compelled to say yes or no to some vital issue of life.[51] If what the preacher has said in the sermon is a matter of life and death, then the conclusion will unfold forcefully out of the content rather than as something imposed on the sermon.

There are guidelines to bear in mind. First, the conclusion of a sermon should be suitable for that particular sermon only and not for any other. Second, the preacher must carefully assess whether the conclusion is true to the theme and content of the sermon. Third, the purpose for that particular conclusion should fit into the larger aim sought in ending sermons. Fourth, it is better to end the sermon when people are still paying attention than to conclude when you have lost almost everybody. Fifth, only in rare circumstances should the preacher hint that the sermon is about to conclude. No one should mistake a sermon conclusion for anything else. Sixth, allow the Holy Spirit to intervene in ways unknown to you. In those circumstances be flexible and let the sermon end the way you had not planned. Seventh, in some cases the conclusion should suggest the way forward. But the most important thing to remember is that the listeners are central to the choices we make in concluding a sermon.

A Cluster of Skills

This section deals with a number of skills and matters the preacher should be aware of. The brief manner in which most of these will be dealt with here does not imply that such techniques are in any way less significant compared to those already discussed.

A. Preaching Without Notes. Authors from the West make different suggestions about what the preacher could do in the pulpit for the actual delivery of sermons. They are generally accommodative in that one could do whatever is comfortable—from preaching without notes to using a full manuscript or scant notes. For the preacher in Africa there is no choice but to polish the skill of preaching without relying on a full manuscript. By preaching without notes I don't mean that there should not be anything on the podium. Preaching without notes for me means that the preacher is not glued to whatever has been taken into the pulpit. It should be scary to any preacher to imagine that while you are looking down at your notes the congregation will be staring at the top of your head. No matter what arguments are put forward, for the African preacher preaching without notes is the most successful approach.

African traditional culture did not rely on the written word. Even today in rural Africa it is the spontaneous spoken word that still dominates forms of communication. In their daily lives and experiences Africans do not use prepared notes to speak. Using notes in the pulpit, then, turns the preacher into an alien from outer space in the midst of the African people. The circumstances in which the African preacher finds him or herself often dictates that notes cannot be easily used for preaching purposes. For example, it is common for the African preacher to preach in complete darkness. This often happens at funerals where people are usually seated outside the homestead of the deceased for evening prayers. Even at revivals at camp meetings the lighting systems can be undependable at times. In addition, people sit in all directions so much that the preacher must move from one end to the other. This is true when the church building is small and some people have to sit outside. The preacher must be free to move to where those people are.

Maybe one of the most important reasons for a preacher to be free from using notes is that somehow Africans, at least in Zimbabwe, associate speaking the truth with speaking without notes. A reporter interviewed some people after a political rally in one of the townships in Zimbabwe about the impressions they had of the speaker. One interviewee remarked that because the speaker did not read from a prepared speech, that in itself was a sign of being honest and that the speech came from the speaker's heart.[52]

B. Eye Contact. When I was growing up I remember how we would remark to each other, "Why are you looking at me like that?" The other one would retort, "How have you seen me looking at you?" The point is that people look at each other for different reasons, but underlying most of the eye contact is communication. In African homes children know that when parents look at them in a certain way in the presence of visitors, they are being told to go and play outside. Eyes carry with them messages that can be easily deciphered by those familiar with the signals.

Through eye contact preaching can become a two-way communication. By looking broadly at the congregation the alert preacher could discern not only what the physical eye is seeing, but that which only the intuitive can observe. Intuitive visual contact can help the preacher determine whether the sermon is engaging the hearer. There are always generous individuals in congregations who will smile, giggle, or even laugh openly, ululate, frown, or display some other overt expression for the benefit of the preacher. It takes awhile to get there but a seasoned preacher can even gauge from looking at the congregation if they want you to explain a point a bit more, wish for you to go on, or beg for you to stop. Keeping in touch with the congregation through eye contact is a skill beneficial to the preacher.

There are some matters to consider on eye contact. Looking at someone is different from staring at a person. Thank God, there are almost no opportunities for the preacher to stare at anyone during the sermon. But members of the congregation have all the opportunity in the world to stare at the preacher. I have observed in my preaching experiences that while the elderly avoid looking too much at the preacher, youths and young adults grab the opportunity to look the preacher in the eyes. The African culture regards looking into the eyes of a respected person, such as a preacher and an elder, as impolite. The youth and the young adults are not necessarily impolite when they look at the preacher but are merely manifesting a culture in transition.

It is tempting for the preacher to respond to the many signals one observes from among the members of the congregation. Do you ask why that young man is shaking his head in open disapproval (I had such an experience at Old Mutare Mission)? Do you smile back in response to that happy, broad smile from one member who even extends a handshake to the other sitting next to her? Outwardly, the preacher should appear to be doing nothing, but inwardly he or she should respond appropriately to match the feedback. Eye contact for the preacher should embrace all the pastoral activities. McNulty grasped this point when he urged preachers to develop a "good eye." When the preacher develops a good eye, he or she will see what must be seen and will then say what must be said.[53]

C. Voice. When I was young I thought that holiness resided in the preacher's voice. Pastors changed the way they spoke the moment they entered the pulpit to preach. Blessed are those preachers who have gone through voice therapy and received training in use of the vocal cords. Most African preachers have not been fortunate to get such training. What everyone could do, however, is ensure that their voice is loud enough that people can hear. It is helpful to ask the congregation whether you are being heard. At times, the preacher can see people in strained postures indicating that he or she is not being heard. A microphone may only add to the problems. Because it is so important that the preacher's voice be projected well, the preacher should attempt to be acquainted with such arrangements before the actual preaching moment.

Most African preachers have no problem raising their voices. People call each other from afar in villages and in the fields, thereby getting used to the need to raise voices. The preacher should aim at preaching in a normal conversational voice with some life behind it. Varying voice pitch is a skill every preacher should learn. Telling a story in the sermon usually helps to lower the voice for the preacher with a problem of high pitch. Telling a story demands that the voice be adjusted accordingly. One way to help the preacher improve the voice for preaching is to occasionally listen to one's own tape-recorded sermons. Be courageous in asking others or only your family members to give you constructive criticism. Remember, we have just talked about preaching in concrete terms. When preaching involves some characters in the biblical text or in a story, try to speak imaginatively as those characters might have spoken, shouted, or cried out. If successful, such creativity brings an aura of reality to the sermon. All we can say is that since preaching depends heavily on the use of spoken words, the preacher's voice is a crucial component in the delivery of the sermon.

D. Direct or Indirect Communication. Preachers are usually advised that their sermons be targeted to that particular congregation. There is, however, the other side of the coin that the preacher must be aware of. Using "you" too much in a sermon may elicit defensive mechanisms from the whole congregation or among those who perceive that they are the target of the sermon. Successful preaching is invitational in its approach. The preacher still says with Hosea, "Rejoice not, O Israel!" (Hos. 9:1), and later on cajoles, "Return, O Israel, to the LORD your God . . ." (Hos. 14:1). It is interesting and instructive to the preacher that in the Bible the concluding message from the prophets is always one of reconciliation rather than alienation.

Our preaching should use those skills that allow the prophetic word to be announced and underwritten by God's everlasting love for humanity. Fred Craddock's concept of "overhearing the gospel" is that people listen to the sermon and assimilate it positively when the approach is indirect.[54] An example is when a preacher gives a children's sermon in the presence of parents. The adults relax and pay close attention to what is being said because they believe that the sermon is not meant for them. Or closer to our own experience, think of how we listen in to a conversation in which we are not directly involved. In most cases if the talk is interesting we listen carefully because there is no pressure to think in advance what point to raise to counter the other speaker. Not every sermon will accommodate indirect communication, but it pays to be alert to such possibility.

E. Gestures. Rarely do we see an African speaking in a rigid position without gesturing. In some cases, the gestures culminate into the dramatization or mimicking what is being represented in speech. What can be said about gestures is that they need to be natural and mesh smoothly with the idea being emphasized. The fewer and more meaningful gestures are, the better, otherwise they become a hindrance in communication. The preacher will do well to focus more on welcoming gestures than anything else. "Gestures, when employed, should be like the striking of a hammer on the head of a nail. It should drive the thought in . . .", asserted W. B. Riley.[55]

When we preach contextually we should take time to study gestures that have distinctive meaning to our culture. In African culture like in any other, there are gestures that display a sense of authority. Putting one's hands in one's pockets is a gesture of disrespect among the Shona people. Waving one's hand is associated with cheerful greetings and a good message. Thus gestures should be expressed in the context of the congregational experience.

F. Mannerisms. Individual preachers have all sorts of mannerisms that they display in the pulpit. The irony about mannerisms or habits is that they are usually unknown to the preacher. Mannerisms are not skills as such but when they are not offensive and add some positive impact to the sermon, they help in the total posturing of the preacher. In the technological age of video cameras preachers should do everything possible to see themselves preaching at least once. If that is impossible, instead ask a few people to give you feedback on your mannerisms in the pulpit.

G. Humour. Africans are humorous people in everyday life. They are humorous even at funerals where close friends, *sahwiras* (for Murewa area in Zimbabwe), and daughters-in-laws imitate some of the characteristics of the deceased. In his service as a missionary in Zaire, now the Democratic Republic of Congo, L. Arden Almquist noticed the widespread sense of humour among the Africans there.[56] Humour has a number of positive functions, one of which is to ease a tense situation and thereby prepare the people to listen to what follows. More so there is something spiritually uplifting about laughter.

Every preacher must be aware of the possible consequences of the humour. I have heard humour about other ethnic groups from preachers. In times when we are encouraging building bridges among different groups of people, such humour is in bad taste.

Homileticians give different advice on the use of humour in the pulpit. Such guidelines often include not using humour in the introduction and in the conclusion. Further, preachers are advised that there are subjects too sacred for a humorous touch, such as hope, faith, and prayer. For preaching, people should be able to perceive the higher goal, the sacred in and through the humour.[57] Humour should be grafted into the sermon in the most natural way, especially when it can easily blend with the sermon. I have observed that it is easier for naturally humorous people to use humour in the pulpit than those who are not of that inclination ordinarily.

One great preacher from Zimbabwe who used humour effectively in his preaching is Bishop Abel T. Muzorewa. His humour came to the listener well wrapped up in the message. It is up to the listener to decide what to do with it, because the preacher does not show any sign that he intended the statement to be humorous. I recall a sermon the Bishop preached at Dorowa at a revival. He asked the audience what they would do if a family in their village announced that they had decided to eat cow dung for the rest of their lives. He was preaching on the importance of making careful decisions within God's offer of free will. People broke into laughter, but none could miss the message. Humour is not just an utterance when coming from the pulpit. The use of humour in preaching demands a high degree of sensitivity on the part of the preacher. A sermon can easily falter as a result of misplaced sense of humour.

Plagiarism

Plagiarism, the dishonest practice of stealing and using other people's material, ideas, and creativity without acknowledgement, is usually raised in academic circles. It is not all that easy in preaching to be clear about where to draw the boundaries. If one goes to a worship service to hear a sermon about what has never been said before, it is advisable to stay home. But if the intention is to hear what one has heard before and hopes that at this particular occasion the preacher will say it differently, that is a reasonable expectation. So where does the issue of plagiarism come in? A few guidelines are in order. First, the honest preacher should listen to his or her conscience and determine whether the information could be used without acknowledging the source. Second, would the preacher feel comfortable if the originator of the idea or ideas were to walk in through the door during the sermon? Third, acknowledgement in a sermon need not be elaborate. A statement mentioning that you heard this interesting idea from a preacher and thought of developing it this or that way will suffice. Fourth, it is a sign of maturity on the part of the preacher to give others credit due to them. Church members travel and visit each other and attend worship services in more different places than preachers normally have the opportunity to. These members have probably listened to the same sermon by different preachers without any of them acknowledging that they borrowed from someone else.

Indeed, some sermons should be heard by many people in different places with minor adjustments. I imagine that many preachers would grant permission, if asked, to their colleagues to preach that preacher's full sermon. The issue of plagiarism in the pulpit is more real in the African context where pastors are usually overloaded with work as we have already stated. Maybe it is not so much the need to give credit to others that matters, but how such a habit can affect the preacher's sense of hard work in regarding sermons and creativity.

Congregational Dynamics

In discussing exegesis we made reference to the need to know and understand the congregation. That level of understanding deals with the socioeconomic and the environmental surroundings of a given congregation. What we refer to here are the nuances silently put into motion as the sermon progresses. We have already made similar implication under the section on eye contact with the congregation. Here our focus is on understanding subtle issues that arise as people listen to the sermon, and conversely making it incumbent on the preacher to develop skills to be able to discern such dynamics. Of interest is the observation that Ralph Lewis made that the minister preaches at least four sermons simultaneously. The four sermons are the auditory, the visual, the emotional, and the intellectual. All four correspond to the different modes of language. The auditory is heard through the language of sound, the visual through the language of bodily actions, the emotional through the language of feeling, and the intellectual through the language of the mind.[58] A skilled preacher will intentionally assess whether the sermon is balanced in all the four languages and do something to remedy any deficiency.

George E. Sweazey noted something with which most people who also have listened to sermons would probably agree. He said listeners do not follow a sermon at a steady pace. Instead, they come and go mentally in paying attention to the preacher.[59] My own experience in listening to sermons is that at times the wandering of my mind is engendered by the preached sermon itself. An idea in the sermon triggers a series of associations in my mind, followed by a realization that the preacher has already covered much ground during my silent moments of reflection. There are some obstacles that listeners normally bring to the worship event. There could be general lack of interest, apathy, lack of commitment, and demands from family pressures. Adding to those congregational obstacles are those of the preacher, such as lack of time and lack of training.[60] All these factors coalesce to create barriers that hinder smooth connection in preaching between the preacher and the congregation.

It is important for the preacher to remember the obvious—that preaching is done for the purpose of communicating the gospel to listeners who usually voluntarily come to hear that message. That the decision to come and hear the gospel has been made is evident, what is always not predictable is whether they will actually hear when the sermon is preached. All the discussions about different skills at the disposal of the preacher are meant to be aids in facilitating the communication and hearing of the gospel. When all is said, we might as well still say with Jesus Christ, not in despair but with hope, that those who have ears, let them hear.

Chapter 4

Can Preaching Be Taught?

When the question, can preaching be taught? comes up, there are a lot of assumptions behind it. Let us look at some of those assumptions. One assumption is that preaching is too complex and sacred for anyone to understand it enough to teach others. A second assumption is that since preaching is too sacred and complex for anyone to be able to teach others, there is a God-given means through which people learn how to preach. A third assumption is that since both the instructor and the leaner bow in obedience before the Word of God in the sermon, no one can assume the role of the teacher. Fourth, there are issues and aspects about preaching that defy any approach in the teaching/learning process. And more assumptions could be raised about whether preaching can be taught.

This chapter is based on the firm belief that preaching can be taught. What we need to do is to expand our understanding of the environment in which the teaching/learning processes of preaching take place as well as its nature. Rather than confine ourselves to a traditional classroom with students and teacher, our horizon should include the whole environment as both the teacher and the location for learning preaching. The formal classroom can equip students of preaching with tools to understand the ever-expanding environment in a meaningful way. In the African situation, where many preachers do not have access to formal training, questions about teaching and learning preaching assume an added significance.

Since those without training can preach, it mistakenly follows that there is no need for learning the intricacies of preaching. That is not the end of the questions regarding teaching/learning preaching. Another question regarding instruction is not how these preachers are taught, but how do people learn to preach?[1] It is an important question because knowing how people learn a particular discipline determines the method of instruction.

In addition to the above, this chapter will have as its central trajectory the way preaching can best be taught in the African context in light of what has already been discussed in this book. One cannot claim to develop an independent theory about teaching and learning preaching distinctively for Africa alone. Even with that understanding, we can explore the teaching/learning process of the African situation in a way that makes it contextually meaningful.

Teaching Principles

In theological schools, teaching principles of education are assumed rather than articulated. The way the instructor was taught in a given theological discipline is most likely to be the way he/she in turn teaches the students. One problem is the possibility of perpetuating outdated methods of instruction, despite great strides made through research in improving teaching methodologies. My proposition is that teaching homiletics demands that the instructor be aware of the diverse but basic teaching principles. Homiletics involves multi-sensory awareness both on the part of the preacher and the listener. It is therefore incumbent on the instructor to teach in a way that involves the whole person. The methods of preaching ought to be reflected in the methods involved in the teaching and learning process.

The basic principles of teaching homiletics that I have in mind come from Bloom's Taxonomy of Learning Domains:, cognitive, affective, and psychomotor. It is the responsibility of the instructor to determine where in preaching each domain comes into focus. Further, the question, what is preaching? must guide the development of goals and objectives for the teaching/learning process. If we say that preaching is communication, it follows that to learn preaching, one must understand the dynamics of communication. The tendency is to confine our attention to the description of what preaching is without taking note of the implications of the description for the teaching/learning process. The point is that one's understanding of what preaching is does shape the broader goals and objectives for teaching and learning. Another way of putting it is that if we say preaching should be done contextually, conversely by implication we say that the teaching/learning process must be carried out in a given context. To say that African preachers must use idioms, proverbs, and other speech forms pertaining to the African situation does not tell the whole story. In reality the syllabus should be designed in a way that specifically shows where and how students will be taught to develop, gather, and use such speech forms in preaching.

The Main Perspective

There are some determinant perspectives within which the teaching/learning of preaching must be done. First is the theological perspective where the focus is on the development of a theology of preaching.[2] Each student must be given the opportunity to search and come to grips with why he or she must preach. Students come to the learning process with some ideas about the theological undergirding for preaching. Building on what is already shaped, the student will be exposed to further thoughts that have supported this church's ministry for ages.

Second is the ecclesiological perspective that preaching belongs to the church. Unlike other theological disciplines that can easily be pursued to quench intellectual thirst, preaching can only be studied in a meaningful way if both the preacher and the learner are constantly aware of their partnership with the already preaching church.

Third is the cultural perspective that takes into consideration the particular context in which preaching occurs. A sermon is specific and unique mainly because it is developed with a unique group of people in mind at a given point in time. A fourth perspective of communication is this: Preaching ultimately demands that the taste of the pudding is in the eating. Or using a Shona proverb, *Totenda maruwa* dzawa *shakata*, meaning, "We shall be thankful when the flowers of the tree turn to be fruits (*shakata*)." In our context it implies whatever one teaches and learns in preaching are just "flowers" until the context is communicated to the congregation.

It is, however, not enough to group these perspectives without alerting the student to reflect on the meaning and context of each perspective. There will be no valid African preaching in an environment where African theology is still held in limbo. What, for an example, should be the Christology for an African pulpit in a situation where African theologians are still in search of approval? Consequently, the teaching of preaching in Africa cannot take either the theology of preaching or the preached theology for granted. The hermeneutic process for the African student of preaching is cumbersome. The process involves not only the selected biblical texts, but a quest for an authentic theology germane to the African situation.

Coming to the ecclesiological perspective, we wonder about the identity of the African church to which the student of preaching will be called upon to proclaim the gospel. Again the question of the identity of the church in Africa is still at a suggestive level of theological reflection. But some ideas are promising such as Bénézet Bujo's suggestion of a "Eucharistic Ecclesiology" for the African Church. The African Church should be centred on the Eucharist as "a life-giving ecclesial meal." Such a church will compel its leaders to meet people's needs and preach a gospel that seeks to eradicate poor conditions of living.[3] One's image of the church influences the preaching of the gospel. Thus teaching preaching in Africa should be eclectic and take into consideration the unfinished business regarding the meaning of what is the African church.

The cultural perspective is all-embracing for the teaching of homiletics in Africa. This book is an attempt to put the ministry of preaching under the African cultural microscopic. Seminary education in Africa has not yet merged itself fully in the surrounding culture. As one writer put it, "Among the tragic consequences of the current seminary system in Africa is the extent to which the indigenous clergy are apt to be alienated from their own cultural heritage."[4] One major reason for this alienation is that in most cases Africans go through education being taught in non-indigenous languages, French, Portuguese, and English. It is well known that the language of study is powerful in shaping one's worldview. Further, books and other resources used in African institutions of learning are not prepared with Africans in mind. The lack of confidence on the part of curriculum planners to revamp the whole seminary education to reflect the African context is another major reason for such alienation of seminarians from their culture. In light of this discussion, the need to approach the cultural perspective in a comprehensive manner in the teaching/learning of homiletics becomes urgent.

I have added communication as the fourth perspective for obvious reasons. Preaching is by nature a communicative discipline. It is through preaching that the accumulated knowledge learned in various theological disciplines is publicly communicated to the gathered church. I am also convinced that irrespective of how much one masters the theories of homiletics and applies them in preparing to preach, a sermon can still falter if the actual approach of communicating the message is ineffective. Writing about the teaching/learning of preaching in Japan, Tsuneaki Kato pointed out that the problem confronting students is how to communicate in an oral language what they have acquired through exegesis in a way understandable to the congregation.[5] Communication is important and must be seriously considered in the process of teaching/learning preaching.

Approaches in Teaching/Learning: Selected Topics

In this section I will suggest how we could go about the teaching/learning process of some of the themes of this book. Here the focus is on contextual thrusts that the instructor and the learner could highlight.

A. Contextual Preaching. I have learned the hard way that when left to themselves, students do not usually take the contextual path as they study theological disciplines. It is important to be intentional in teaching preaching in ways that are contextual to the African situation. A study of terms such as *adaptation, inculturation, indigenization, contextualization,* and *skenosis,* will be helpful if students don't have this background already.[6] What is usually forgotten is that doing theological studies contextually is a discipline in itself. Students may not be grounded in how to go about it on their own, and merely urging them to be contextual may not be adequate. This means that the teaching/learning process must provide space for thoughts and methods that reflect the African context.

If the African contextual life revolves around community, the teaching/learning methods must deliberately encourage a communal approach to life. Since preaching is not a private ministry, students should be encouraged to work together in groups eager to help each other. Pastors in the field tend to work in separate enclaves, something that can be traced to their individual approach to learning during their seminary days. It is indeed one way of contextualizing seminary education to remove all aspects of theological education that encourage unnecessary competition among students.

B. What Is Preaching? We need to revisit the usual way of presenting a prepared lecture with the hope of informing students what is meant by preaching. Don M. Wardlaw says that when conducting seminars on preaching he begins by getting into the pulpit to preach, with a disclaimer that he is not setting an example for the participants to emulate.[7] Unfortunately, learners tend to view what the instructor or leader of the seminar does as setting the tone and example to follow. I would suggest that in a homiletics class students should begin the lesson on "What is preaching?" by preaching. I usually check with my students to find out how many among them have never preached before. The number is usually one or two in a class of at least twelve students. Some denominations require that candidates for the ministry must first become local preachers. Asking them to preach and discuss their experiences in a collegial atmosphere will help them become more confident of their preaching.

When theoretical discussion follows the act of preaching, the meaning is clear. Even when we find it helpful to explore the principles and the practice of contextual preaching in separate discussions (as I have done here in these two volumes), the actual teaching/learning process must reunite the two.Students learn by doing and then reflecting on images of proclaiming the gospel in the African context. Information about preaching can best be understood when studied against the background of actual practice.

If as noted earlier, preaching reflects the preacher's personality, then the question about what is a distinctively African personality becomes important. Africans have a corporate personality ingrained in traditional culture. This corporate personality manifests itself in the desire to build communities of people rather than isolating themselves, and is expressed through an overflowing sense of hospitality. Think of what preaching could be when the preacher naturally projects a hospitable mood to the congregation. What is understood in African culture as good personality and character? Rather than gloss over these ideas, students of homiletics must grapple with such issues as they relate personality to preaching.

C. The Portrait of the Preacher. It is the responsibility of every preacher to identify the image and implications for preaching that he/she would like to follow. Class participation could begin by centering on sharing one's understanding of the call. What does it mean for the preacher to be called to preach? Reflections should not be distanced from the lived experiences of the students. Let them share their stories in a relaxed non-judgmental atmosphere.

Students should be made aware that most preachers do not arrive at churches fully formed; rather, they experience a journey of becoming who they want to be. Most books on homiletics do an excellent job of describing what the character of a preacher should be, but say little or nothing about how one becomes a pilgrim throughout a preaching career. This is the point when the teaching/learning of preaching must address the spiritual demands of ministry. As students read about images of the preacher, they can then relate them to their context. What does it mean to them to be separated and be underwater with the mermaid, *nzuzu*? Could they think of other images of being separated and consecrated for bigger responsibilities? Although a preacher is not a chief in the village, the traditional rites of how chiefs are selected and set apart could be a source of inspiration. Images empower, inspire, and paint a concrete picture of an idea that could easily dissipate into abstract thought. A search of such images of the preacher from within the African context could be energizing.

D. Preparing to Preach. Rather than merely writing notes on the chalkboard about how one prepares to preach, a better approach is to ask students to begin to develop homiletical resources. They can begin to take notes and keep ideas for future development. This approach will cultivate the eye and ear of the preacher, something on which they will depend for the rest of their preaching careers. Again the intentional interweaving of theory and practice should characterize each lesson. In African context the instructor should inculcate the attitude that preaching is hard work, and that those who are successful approach this ministry with reverence inspired by the sense of the holy.

We have noted that Africans have a talent for impromptu speaking, but if they think that there is no need for serious preparation it can become the bane of their preaching career. Too much work for pastors can also lead to lack of close attention in preparing sermons. The fact that lay people without training do well at preaching can mislead the pastor to think that anyone can stand up and preach with little preparation. Hence, there is a need to shape proper attitudes toward working hard in preparing to preach. This working hard should not be separated from moments of prayer and solid belief in the Holy Spirit. Students must be given the opportunity to share about living lives based on prayer, belief, and trust in the efficacy of the Holy Spirit.

One other area that needs more attention in the teaching/learning of preaching in Africa is exegesis and hermeneutics. Here again, both the instructor and the student must wear contextual lenses. Teaching exegesis and hermeneutics for preaching in Africa should not end with the traditional method of exegeting a biblical text. African students in theological education in general and in the study of homiletics in particular should be made conscious of the hermeneutics of suspicion. Basically the paradigm of hermeneutics of suspicion begins on the assumption that every text has a mask that must be removed in order to reach to the truth. The hermeneutics of suspicion extols doubt be removed in order to reach to the truth. The hermeneutics of suspicion extols doubt over uncritical acquiescence in the given interpretation.[8]

Hermeneutics of suspicion for the African theologian and preacher should mean that the text is approached on the assumption that the African condition and experience has been left out. The Western world has predominantly fed its norms into the ways the biblical text is generally interpreted today. This exercise may begin by tracing the African motif in the Bible and trying to discern the meaning of those texts for the African contemporary church. If the Bible has been used to marginalize the people of African descent it is now time to uplift and empower through the proclamation of the gospel those who have been disadvantaged.

Apart from exegesis and hermeneutics the African student of preaching should be enticed to see biblical interpretation as interesting and rewarding. Through it students search texts for intriguing information. They can then share their findings in class and relate what information could be equally of interest to the congregation and what might be left out. Imagine the exegetical findings that St. Paul never wrote that "nobody is perfect" or "we were all sinners," but that these words were written by Petronius, "a wicked friend of the equally wicked Emperor Nero" who wanted to justify all vices.[9] Such information is likely to encourage students of preaching to go through this painstaking search that ends up enriching their biblical understanding.

Further preparation for preaching for the African preacher should rely considerably on pastoral contacts. Africans value time spent in the company of each other. Most African families still take time to engage in meaningful conversations revealing some aspects of life experiences they might be going through. Helge Beden Nielsen has stated the need for linking pastoral care and homiletics: "In times where pastoral care is neglected we often see that the sermons tend to be abstract bodies so to speak, without connection with human experience."[10] I personally experimented with the conclusion that a pastor who visits parishioners on Saturday (exact day is not important) will have a full church on Sunday and found it to be true. An instructor of homiletics in Africa should urge students to closely combine their preaching with pastoral visitation and general care of members.

E. What to Preach? In teaching students about preaching, it is important to make them aware that the major source of problems in preaching is not how to preach but what to preach. It is unfortunate that studies in homiletics lean more on how to preach than on what to preach.

In Africa the question concerning what to preach is essential because the gospel to be proclaimed should be shaped by trends in African theological reflection. The hermeneutics of suspicion is urged upon African preachers on the premise that the gospel of the missionary church in Africa needs revisiting. Africa urgently needs a holistic message that incorporates salvation for the whole person. Sharing this understanding of the significance of what to preach, Bujo pointed out: "All Christian preaching must help to restore the confidence of the people of Africa in their cultural heritage."[11] African economic debt is discussed by foreigners who protest for humanitarian reasons while the church in Africa goes about its business as usual. African preachers should be challenged to raise these issues in their sermons for the benefit of their people. Africa is a continent where human rights are not guaranteed for the majority of people. Freedom in Jesus Christ should relate existentially to these issues of fear and insecurity that confront the African people on a daily basis. The baby Jesus of today can no longer be taken to Africa as a refuge from Herod's persecution. It is the responsibility of the African student of preaching to understand the issues and begin to develop sermons that address problems that call upon the Holy Spirit to guide the people in solving them.

In analyzing the Sermon on the Mount, Manfred Josuttis argues that the mountain is a symbol of the authority every preacher is endowed with upon entering the pulpit. The pulpit is not the place for everyday talk about the existing sociopolitical and economic issues. "Whoever enters the pulpit speaks with authority only after having mastered the language of the mountain," said Josuttis. He went on, "In the pulpit there is no need to repeat what is said over and over again in the everyday world of church and society, of ideology and morals . . . Whoever dares to enter the pulpit must transcend the insight of all theological, psychological, pedagogical, and political theories."[12] Africa needs sermons that are more than a mere repeat of what is heard on the street. Students should be challenged to think through the content of their sermons in light of the lost hope, poverty, and insecurity around issues that characterize the African context.

F. How to Preach? Language is a key element in preaching and any teaching/learning process must highlight that. In addition to commentaries and other tools for biblical studies, a homiletics student in Africa should posses a dictionary in the indigenous language, a collection of proverbs and idioms, and some African novels. Further, I suggest that one of the practices to be urged on students is to attend the courts and observe how chiefs and elders conduct themselves in speech.

Depending on one's denominational tradition, the use of song in preaching to punctuate the sermon is generally welcomed by the congregation. African students of homiletics should be encouraged to use song in their training sessions when appropriate. It is a rare African group of people who will disapprove of well-synchronized hymn singing during preaching. Writing about the singing of the Zulu people of South Africa, one writer called their music "this gift of Zululand so beautiful in its many tones and modes of expression."[13] Africans are a singing people whose music expresses all aspects of life. Thus the use of song in the proclamation of the gospel is one of the many ways of contextualizing preaching in Africa.

One of the best methods of teaching students how to preach is through micro-teaching methods adapted to preaching. Micro-teaching is a model of teaching in which a student practices a set of skills under observation. For micro-preaching the student prepares and presents a sermon focusing on selected skills that the class will critique. Where possible the best outcomes can be yielded if the presentation is videotaped and then replayed for critique. Prepared questions could be used to check on skills such as eye contact, voice projection, use of manuscript, use of various forms of language, introduction, conclusion, and so forth.

The teaching/learning of how to preach demands a field-based approach in which congregations are involved. I am aware that in the African context it is not easy to find congregations willing to critique students' sermons. For them the preached word of God should not be subjected to scrutiny. I remember Reverend Jakazi, an African pastor at St. John's Anglican Church in Mutare, who attempted to involve the congregation in responding to his sermons. On one occasion I was present when he asked members of the congregation to remain behind to critique his sermon. Although the response was minimal, I appreciated his effort at involving the congregation in his preaching.

At one time I was involved in a preaching workshop for the women's group at St. Peter's United Methodist Church, Mutare. For the closing sessions I asked one woman to preach and the others to critique. There was initial resistance that thawed when I explained that to critique a sermon did not belittle the Word of God in any way. Much work can be done in the field to train students in how to preach. We must cultivate and orient congregations to become partners in training pastors to preach.

Observation is another method of teaching/learning how to preach. Students should avail themselves of opportunities to observe others preach. There are two types of observation: purposeful and emergent. In purposeful observation the observer has a preplanned strategy of what is to be observed, with room for other factors to be included. In emergent observation there is preplanning in the sense that the learner is aware that he/she will observe an event but the process is open ended. What is to be observed is not predetermined.[14] As students attend church services, funeral, weddings, and other occasions they could use one of the two methods to observe sermons.

G. Sermon Analysis. Observation and sermon critique are components of sermon analysis. Details of this sermon analysis have been described in Why We Preach, the first book in this study. Students of preaching should be familiar with this method as a teaching/learning process. We have already noted that African preachers don't usually write out their sermons. For the purpose of analysis, tape-recording or video-recording can be used. The advantage of analyzing sermons by other preachers is that students are more relaxed and open in their responses than they are when critiquing each other. A student can focus on areas that he/she feels there is need to polish some skills.

Self-Evaluation

Anyone who wants to be effective in preaching must learn the art of self-evaluation. The first and most important requirement is to be humble before God and people in acknowledging that a preacher is a learner throughout his/her career. Self-evaluation can take place as one openly requests feedback from friends or family members. The use of a tape recorder or video recorder can be helpful in following up some aspects of the delivery. Hearing one's own voice is usually surprising. What is required is to be honest with oneself in endorsing strengths and pointing out areas for improvement.

Continuing Education

The best and most successful outcome of teaching homiletics is for students to develop an intrinsic curiosity for sustained learning beyond seminary days. I remember a comment one of my homiletics students made at the end of the last lesson in the semester at Africa University. As I bade the class farewell and wished them well in their examinations, Almedia Lemba commented, "So you think we can now preach?" I could not answer. I wish I could tell the student that he could for sure preach, but that is an area shrouded with mystery and uncertainties only assured by the never-failing presence of the Holy Spirit. But one thing all students of preaching can do is to continually study their discipline.

Continuing education in the African context should go beyond organized workshops and other planned formal settings of learning. African pastors should be resourceful in how they continue to learn. The sense of communal life among Africans should be transformed into reality. Pastors could gather and share books among themselves. Congregations could pull resources and purchase books that their pastors could share in their fraternal organizations. It is unfortunate that Africans write so much about the place community holds in their lives without saying how that community-centred life is needed today and can be utilized. In Zimbabwe there is talk of implementing *Zunde raMambo* (the chief's field), which existed in traditional culture. Everyone in the village was required to work in this *Zunde* (field). Crops from the field were stored and made available to those in need free of charge. The ways such a field could be managed may change in modern days but the basic idea behind the practice, caring through sharing, does not change. I say this because the church is one institution in Africa that can take the lead in showing that people can share, care for each other, and work together. In Africa rather than merely complaining about a lack of resources preachers learn to share ideas and resources.

Continuing education for the African preacher also means that when possible each pastor should worship and hear sermons in other churches. It is rewarding to hear another preacher handle a text you have also preached on in a completely different way. Imagination in preaching is usually stimulated by listening to the way others use fantastic embellishments in their sermons. If a pastor is not preaching in his/her church and there is no reason to be present, worshipping at a neighbouring church can provide personal enrichment. It may also happen that pastors don't worship deeply in their congregations because they are under pressure to oversee everything. Thus worshipping with another congregation may turn out to be worthwhile not only for personal growth in preaching but also for spiritual enrichment.

Pastors shy away from leading Bible studies in their churches because they are not aware of the close link between such an activity in Christian education and preaching. To be sure, Bible study does not in itself guarantee improved preaching but it has positive contributions to a pastor's preaching career. A pastor will have an opportunity to read and listen to biblical texts outside the context of sermon preparation. Further, the pastor will learn from the ideas of the parishioners as they share how the texts speak to them.

One time I led a group of church members in discussing tithing as a form of giving mandated by the Bible. One woman in the group, Mrs. Mawoyo, said that in her view a tithe is *mombe yeumai*, that is, a cow given to the mother of the bride as part of *lobola* in Shona culture. This cow is sacred and highly valued and every bridegroom tries to see that the mother-in-law gets it without delay. This is a wonderful idea of contextualizing the teaching of the tithe that I, the pastor, had never thought of. Bible study and other learning activities done together with church members could provide rich arenas and resources for continuing education as an everyday activity.

Wendland sees the need for a combined effort in Africa where sermons from various regions of the continent could be gathered in transcribed and translated form. Such a collection of sermons could then be analyzed by scholars and practitioners in preaching.[15] The material will readily render itself to case studies as well as comparing parts of Africa. Indeed, this approach will advance the teaching of homiletics on the African continent in seminaries, colleges, and universities. Africa University, through its Faculty of Theology and other regional centres of higher theological education, could take the lead in such a venture. Collected sermons will in the end enable sustainable courses or seminars on African rhetoric in preaching.

Although there are a number of aspects of teaching/learning homiletics I have not dealt with in this chapter, still my hope is that the ideas shared so far will provide a launching pad for further exploration. Teaching and learning have principles that all who teach and learn are better served in following. Equally important are styles that characterize the individual's way of either teaching or learning. It is my hope that suggestions made here have not stultified the sense of creativity that every individual is endowed with.

Chapter 5

Summary

The focus of this book is the practice of preaching in Africa. It is one thing to grasp the theory of how something should be done. It is indeed another to actually do what is expected. In chapter 1 we have dealt with preparing to preach. The point has been made that a number of factors in the African context do not make the process of preparing to preach easy for the preacher. Some of these factors are lack of resources and burdensome workloads. Impromptu speaking—a positive talent in its own—can also hinder the process of preparing sermons. Africans are good at delivering a speech or sermon on short notice. This ability can be misused, leading to an indifferent attitude in preparing sermons and for preaching. Preparing to preach involves a number of issues every preacher must seriously consider. Special attention should be given to exegesis, not merely to follow the traditional processes involved, but for the African preacher to question the legitimacy and primacy of the given interpretations when viewed in the context of the African situation.

For African preachers, the answer to the question, what do you preach? is not a given. Africa demands a special prophetic message that can lead the African listener to say in the end that he or she is afflicted but not destroyed.[1] We have asserted that too much focus on the African ways and means of communicating the gospel at the expense of the nature of the message to be preached, is shortsighted. Preaching as it exists in Africa appears to be oriented to individual salvation. A holistic gospel is needed in Africa. The "what" of preaching needs more attention from homileticians, especially as it pertains to the African context.

When the message is there the next question is how do you preach? With regard to the modes of preaching, African preaching contributes a number of distinctive essentials. Preaching without notes is the normative way of delivering sermons for African preachers. Further, the use of African forms of speech such as proverbs, idioms, song, and storytelling saturated with imagination is germane to the African context where the spoken word is still dominant.

If any headway is to be made in the attempt to contextualize preaching, it follows that how we teach preachers must be germane to the existing African situation. It is an area that begs for collegial spirit among those involved in teaching other theological disciplines. It is futile to urge students of homiletics to be contextual if that is not a well-coordinated intention throughout the curriculum. No matter how much we emphasize the need for doing theology contextually it will be of little use until that clarion call is accompanied with learning resources produced with the African context in mind.

It is my hope that this book will combine with efforts of others and together provide a solid starting point. To be always remembered in good faith in that contextual preaching, or any other method for that matter, does not make the task any easier. Preaching is an act of worship and is accomplished in the context of faith, which must take precedence and above any other context we can imagine.

Notes

Chapter 1: Preparing to Preach

1. I have discussed these and other broad issues related to the preaching task in Zimbabwe. See E. K. Nhiwatiwa, "Preaching Task in Zimbabwe," in Tsuneaki Kato, ed., *Preaching as God's Mission: Studia Homiletica* 2 (Tokyo: Kyo Bun Kwan, 1999): 154–57.
2. Chang Bok Chung, "Preaching Situation in Korean Church," in Tsuneaki Kato, ed., *Preaching as God's Mission*, pp. 136–41. Chung raised a number of issues such as overwork and lack of in-depth knowledge in homiletics that are similar to the African context.
3. Fred B. Craddock, *As One Without Authority* (Nashville: Abingdon Press, 1979), p. 6. See also John Killinger, *Fundamentals of Preaching* (Minneapolis: Fortress Press, 1991), p. 91. Evangelist Wame urges the preacher to "study man" by making regular pastoral visits. See Ernst R. Wendland, *Preaching that Grabs the Heart: A Rhetorical Stylistic Study of the Chichewa Revival Sermons of Shadrack Wame* (Blantyre, Malawi: Christian Literature Association in Malawi, 2000), p. 247.
4. Samuel Proctor, *The Certain Sound of the Trumpet: Crafting a Sermon of Authority* (Valley Forge, PA: Judson Press, 1994), p. 22.
5. Edmund A. Steimle, Charles L. Rice, Morris J. Niedenthal, *Preaching the Story* (Philadelphia: Fortress Press, 1980), p. 161.
6. For these quotations see Charles L. Rice, *The Embodied Word: Preaching as Art and Liturgy* (Minneapolis: Fortress Press, 1991), p. 134.
7. To mention just a few, see O. C. Edwards, Jr., *Elements of Homiletic: A Method for Preparing to Preach* (Collegeville, MN: Pueblo Publishing Company, 1982), p. 22; John Killinger, *Fundamentals of Preaching*, pp. 190–91; and Illion T. Jones, *Principles and Practice of Preaching: A Comprehensive Study of the Art of Sermon Construction* (Nashville: Abingdon Press, 1984), p. 56.
8. The statement was cited by Gardner Taylor in an interview: David Albert Farmer, "Pulpit Laureate and Presidential Favorite: An Interview with Gardner Taylor," in *Pulpit Digest* 77, no. 541 (September/October 1996): 101.
9. Africans offer prayers for a variety of occasions. See John S. Mbiti, *Introduction to African Religion*, 2nd rev. ed. (Oxford: Heinemann Educational Publishers, 1991), pp. 61–63.
10. Illion T. Jones, *Principles and Practice of Preaching*, p. 70.
11. Phillips Brooks, *Lectures on Preaching* (Grand Rapids, MI: Zondervan, n.d.), p. 135.
12. Edgar N. Jackson, *A Psychology for Preaching* (New York: Great Neck Channel Press, 1961), p. 37.

13. Michael Bourdillon, *Religion and Society: A Text for Africa* (Gweru: Mambo Press, 1990), p. 123.
14. Paul Scott Wilson, "Beyond Narrative: Imagination in the Sermons," in Gail O'Day and Thomas G. Long, eds., *Listening to the Word: Studies in Honor of Fred B. Craddock* (Nashville: Abingdon Press, 1993), p. 139.
15. Fred B. Craddock, *Preaching* (Nashville: Abingdon Press, 1985), p. 31.
16. Ernst R. Wendland, *Preaching that Grabs the Heart*, p. 228.
17. Horst Burkle, "Patterns of Sermons from Various Parts of Africa," in David B. Barrett, ed., *African Initiatives in Religion* (Nairobi, Kenya: East African Publishing House, 1971), p. 224.
18. John S. Mbiti, *African Religions and Philosophy*, 2nd ed. (London: Heinemann Educational Books, 1990), p. 22.
19. Ernst R. Wendland, *Preaching that Grabs the Heart*, p. 245.
20. Martin E. Marty, *The Word: People Participating in Preaching* (Philadelphia: Fortress Press, 1984), p. 69.
21. George E. Sweazey, *Preaching the Good News* (Englewood Cliffs, NJ: Prentice-Hall, 1976), p. 33.
22. Robert G. Hughes and Robert Kysar, *Preaching Doctrine: For the Twenty-First Century* (Minneapolis: Fortress Press, 1997), p. 46.
23. Fred B. Craddock, *As One Without Authority*, p. 129.
24. Ibid.
25. For details on the different types of sermon outlines see Jones, *Principles and Practice of Preaching*, pp. 65–77.
26. A report on decision making among the Tswana says that public policy is openly discussed at an assembly open to all the men of the tribe. There is wide consultation. See I. Schapera and John L. Comaroff, *The Tswana*, rev. ed. (London: Kegan Paul International in Association with International African Institute, 1991), pp. 46–47. The East African revival groups adopt "group consensus" as the dominant procedure in making decisions. See Dorothy E. W. Smoker, "Decision-making in East African Revival Movement Groups," in Publishing House, 1971), p. 105.
27. From a summary made by Bourdillon from various studies by M. Bloch especially from "Decision Making in Councils Among the Merina of Madagascar, 1971," in Bourdillon, *Religion and Society*, p. 108.
28. Fred B. Craddock, *Preaching*, p. 216.
29. H. Beecher Hicks, "Bones, Sinews, Flesh and Blood Coming to Life," in Richard Allen Bodey, *Inside the Sermon* (Grand Rapids, MI: Baker Publishing Company, 1990), p. 116.

Chapter 2: What Do You Preach? The Message

1. *The Confessions of St. Augustine*, trans. John K. Ryan, Book 1, chap. 1 (New York: Image Books/Doubleday, 1960), p. 43.

2. Olin P. Moyd, *The Sacred Art: Preaching and Theology in the African-American Tradition*, (Valley Forge, PA: Judson Press, 1995), p. 50.
3. Ralph Lewis, *Persuasive Preaching Today* (Ann Arbor, MI: Abury Theological Seminary, 1979) pp. 151–52. On this note of the importance of the message see also Jones, *Principles and Practice of Preaching*, p. 182.
4. This is the gist of Desmond Tutu's view on African theological reflection, "Whither African Theology," in E. Fashole-Luke et al., eds., *Christianity in Independent Africa* (London, 1978), pp. 364–69, cited by Kwame Bediako, "African Theology," in David F. Ford, *The Modern Theologians: An Introduction to Christian Theology in the Twentieth Century, 2nd ed.* (Malden, MA: Blackwell Publishers, 1997), p. 427.
5. Martin E. Marty, *The Word: People Participating in Preaching*, p. 12.
6. Ibid., pp. 30–31
7. Austin Phelps, quoted in Arthur S. Hoyt, *Vital Elements of Preaching* (New York: The McMillan Co.), p. 117.
8. Arthur S. Hoyt, *Vital Elements of Preaching*, p. 131.
9. Charles F. Kemp, ed., *Pastoral Preaching* (St. Louis: Bethany Press, 1963), p. 12.
10. Ibid., pp. 17–18
11. Webb B. Garrison, *The Preacher and His Audience* (New York: Fleming H. Revell, n.d.), p. 41.
12. Phillips Brooks, *Lectures on Preaching*, p. 126.
13. Reuel L. Howe, *Partners in Preaching: Clergy and Laity in Dialogue* (New York: The Seabury Press, 1967), p. 42.
14. Edward F. Markquart, *Quest for Better Preaching Resources for Renewal in the Pulpit* (Minneapolis: Augsburg Publishing House, 1985), p. 72.
15. Henry H. Mitchell, *Celebration and Experience in Preaching* (Nashville: Abingdon Press, 1990), p. 63.
16. Kenneth R. Ross, ed., *Gospel Ferment in Malawi: Theological Essays* (Gweru: Mambo Press, 1995), p. 84.
17. Ibid., p. 88. Ross found out that the church in Malawi consistently warns its members on the catalogued vices.
18. Jose B. Chipenda, Andre Karamaga, J .N. K. Mugambi, C. K. Omari, eds., *The Church of Africa: Towards a Theology of Reconstruction* (Nairobi: All Africa Conference of Churches, 1991), p. 25.
19. Ross, *Gospel Ferment in Malawi*, pp. 75–78.
20. Ibid.
21. Nelson Mandela, *Long Walk to Freedom: The Autobiography of Nelson Mandela*, abr. and ed. Coco Cachalia and Marc Suttner (Braamfontein, Gauteng, South Africa: Nolwazi Educational Publishers, 1998), p. 148.
22. L. Arden Almquist was a missionary who spent some time working in Zaire, now the Democratic Republic of Congo. He grasped and articulated some values he learned from the Africans in his book *Debtor Unashamed: The Road to Mission Is a Two-Way Street* (Chicago: Covenant Publications, 1993), p. 22.

23. The quotation is from the brochure prepared for the itinerary of Convocation 2000 that was held at the Interdenominational Theological Center, Atlanta, Georgia, under the leadership of Professor Anne Streaty Wimberly.
24. Richard Lischer, "Preaching as the Church's Language," in O'Day and Long, *Listening to the Word*, p. 113.
25. Ivy Ncube, "AIDS Threatens To Wipe Out Settlement," *The Herald*, 6 November 1999, p. 1. There are numerous cases where AIDS or other illnesses are blamed on evil spirits or other superstitious causes that go unreported among the African people in Zimbabwe. This refusal to face reality holds true in other African countries.
26. "N'angas 'recover' owls, snakes, organ from farm workers' houses," *The Herald*, 6 November 1999, p. 1. Such reports of "recovering" mysterious objects are rife throughout towns and rural areas in Zimbabwe.
27. Mugambi, *Critiques of Christianity*, p. 67. Here Mugambi cites the critical views of Mbiti.
28. John W. de Gruchy, "African Theology: South Africa," in Ford, ed., *The Modern Theologians*, p. 449. The Kairos Document was based on prophetic theology that brought church leaders and theologians in apartheid South Africa to formulate a united voice of the church against apartheid.
29. Christine M. Smith, *Preaching as Weeping, Confession, and Resistance: Radical Responses to Radical Evil* (Louisville, KY: Westminster John Knox Press, 1992), p. 1.
30. Ibid., p. 4.
31. Ibid., p. 5.
32. Walter Brueggemann, *Cadences of Home: Preaching among Exiles* (Louisville, KY: Westminster John Knox Press, 1997), p. 78.
33. Martin E. Marty, *The Word: People Participating in Preaching*, p. 11.
34. For the cartoon, see *The Daily News*, 14 April 2000, p. 8. This was a critique of the church for its failure to speak against the violence in and outside the pulpit.
35. "The Church Must Speak Out!" *Zimbabwe Independent*, 14 April 2000, p. 6.
36. Bromley G. Oxman, *Preaching in a Revolutionary Age* (Nashville: Abingdon/Cokesbury Press, 1944), p. 117. The revolutionary age referred to here when atrocities of all kinds were reported.
37. Gardner C. Taylor, *How Shall They Preach?* (Elgin, IL: Progressive Baptist Publishing House, 1977), pp. 78–80. The image of the watchman, found in Ezekiel 33, is a biblical metaphor for the role of the preacher.
38. Richard Lischer, *The Preacher King: Martin Luther King Jr. and the Word that Moved America* (New York: Oxford University Press, 1995), p. 219.
39. Mugambi, ed., *Critiques of Christianity*, p. 15.
40. Markquart, *Quest for Better Preaching*, p. 129.
41. Ross, *Gospel Ferment in Malawi*, p. 85.
42. Elizabeth Achtemeir, *Preaching as Theology and Art* (Nashville: Abingdon Press, 1984), p. 12.

43. David H. C. Read, *Preaching about the Needs of Real People* (Philadelphia: Westminster Press, 1988), p. 35.
44. T. D. Niles, *Preaching the Gospel of the Resurrection* (Philadelphia: The Westminster Press, 1954), p. 87.
45. For a detailed explanation of this method of preaching, see Fred B. Craddock, *Overhearing the Gospel* (Nashville: Abingdon Press, 1978).
46. John W. Conway, "Have Patience—We'll Be in St. Croix Tonight," in McNulty, ed., *Preaching Better*, p. 122.
47. Ibid., p. 124.
48. Charles Hudson, "Preaching to the Living at a Funeral," in McNulty, ed., *Preaching Better*, p. 116.
49. Almquist, *Debtor Unashamed*, p. 29.

Chapter 3: How Do You Preach? A Repertoire of Skills

1. R. E. C. Browne, *The Ministry of the Word* (London: SCM Press, 1976), p. 24.
2. Ibid., p. 79.
3. On inclusive language, see the chapter on "Emancipatory Language" in Marjorie Proctor Smith, *In Her Own Rite: Constructing Feminist Liturgical Tradition* (Nashville: Abingdon Press, 1990), pp. 59–84. See also Hoyt L. Hickman, *A Primer for Church Worship* (Nashville: Abingdon Press, 1984), pp. 36–37.
4. *The Daily News*, 20 April 2000, p. 12.
5. Ibid., p. 13
6. Mercy Amba Oduyoye, *Daughters of Anowa*, p. 55.
7. Onwubiko, *African Thought, Religion and Culture*, p. 30.
8. Ibid., p. 31.
9. Luke Nnamdi Mbefo, *The Reshaping of African Traditions* (Enugu, Nigeria: Spiritan Publications, 1988), p. 80.
10. Alec J. C. Pongweni, *Figurative Language in Shona Discourse: A Study of the Analogical Imagination* (Gweru, Zimbabwe: Mambo Press, 1989), p. 1.
11. Kurewa, *Biblical Proclamation*, p. 22.
12. Mordikai A. Hamutyinei and Albert B. Plangger, *Tsumo-Shumo: Shona Proverbial Lore and Wisdom* (Gweru, Zimbabwe: Mambo Press, 1974), p. 20.
13. Ibid., p. 3.
14. Ibid., p. 4.
15. Ibid., p. 12.
16. Ibid., p. 13.
17. Oduyoye, *Daughters of Anowa*, p. 57.
18. Ibid., p. 12.
19. J. T. Milimo, *Bantu Wisdom* (Lusaka: National Educational Company of Zambia, 1972), p. 116.
20. For these views see Bourdillon, *Religion and Society*, p. 109.

21. Choan-Seng Song, *Third-Eye Theology: Theology in Formation in Asian Settings* (Maryknoll, NY: Orbis Books, 1979), p. 161.
22. Ibid, p. 175.
23. On the view that imagination can be taught, see Paul Scott Wilson, *Imagination of the Heart: New Understanding in Preaching* (Nashville: Abingdon Press, 1988), pp. 15–48. The whole book is focused on how a preacher could be imaginative.
24. Urban T. Holmes III, *Ministry and Imagination* (New York: The Seabury Press, 1976), pp. 97–98.
25. Barbara Brown Taylor, "Preaching the Body," in O'Day and Long, *Listening to the Word*, p. 213.
26. About this uncritical approach to life, see Temba J. Mafico, "Tradition, Faith, and the Africa University," *Quarterly Review* 9, no. 2 (Summer 1998): 37.
27. Edward P. Wimberly, "The Black Christian Experience and the Holy Spirit," *Quarterly Review* 8, no. 2 (Summer 1998): 21. See also similar sentiments in Mitchell, *Celebration*, p. 17.
28. "Use Your Imagination with Your Salads," *Sunday Mail Magazine*, 29 March 1998, p. 13.
29. Scott Paul Wilson, *Imagination of the Heart*, p. 32.
30. Watson Mabona, "You Fool," a sermon preached at Chinyausunzi Church of Christ, Sakubva, Mutare, Zimbabwe, on 22 November 1997. The occasion was an ordination service for Gift Masengwe, who was then a student in the Faculty of Theology at Africa University. Mabona had previously worked in the film industry where he showed some advertising motion pictures in rural areas. No wonder he preached using mental images.
31. Barbara Brown Taylor, "Preaching the Body," in O'Day and Long, *Listening to the Word*, p. 217. See also Lewis, *Persuasive Preaching*, pp. 216–17.
32. Colin Morris, *The Word and the Words*, pp. 124–25.
33. Lischer, *The Preacher King*, p. 122.
34. *The African Synod: Documents, Reflections, Perspectives*, p. 14. The focus was on the analysis of the Church in Africa.
35. Ian Pitt-Watson, A *Primer for Preachers* (Grand Rapids, MI: Baker Book House, 1986), p. 83. See also George M. Bass, "The Story Sermon," *Preaching* 2 (January/February 1987): 33. Bass sees storytelling as most amenable to free and spontaneous preaching.
36. Henry H. Mitchell, *Celebration*, p. 37–38.
37. In Chapter 3 we have already cited references focusing on storytelling as the appropriate method for preaching. See again Holbert, *Preaching*; Rice, *Preaching of the Story*; Bausch, *Storytelling*; and Thomas G. Long, *Preaching and the Literary Forms of the Bible* (Philadelphia: Fortress Press, 1989). Long's book contends that the method of preaching in a given sermon is determined by the literary form of the chosen text. As Wendland noted, Chewa sermons are based on the narrative approach to communicate the gospel. See Wendland, *Preaching that Grabs the Heart*, p. 83. He also pointed out that the inductive method of preaching that has been

recently discovered in the West is an integral aspect of Chewa preaching. See Wendland, *Preaching that Grabs the Heart*, p. 224.

38. "Have you ever heard of Chimanimani Musical Group?" *Parade*, November 1999, p. 63. Chimanimani is a locality in the Eastern border of Zimbabwe. The idea that stories are taught is prevalent among Western homileticians. See Jay O'Callaghan, "Thoughts on Storytelling" in McNulty, ed., *Preaching Better*, p.
39. Francis Bebey, *African Music A People's Art*, trans. Josephine Bennett (Westport, N.Y.: Lawrence Hill & Co., 1975), p. 3.
40. H. W. Turner, *African Independent Church: The Life and Faith of the Church of the Lord (Alandura)*, vol. 2 (Oxford: Clarendon Press, 1967), p. 113.
41. Ndiokwere, *The African Church*, pp. 263–64.
42. Turner, *African Independent Church*, p. 117.
43. Bebey, *African Music*, p. 30. The *mvet* is a musical instrument that storytellers in Cameroon play while narrating communal stories at the marketplace.
44. Craddock, *Preaching*, p. 196. See also Lischer, "Preaching as the Church's Language," in O'Day and Long, *Listening to the Word*, p. 127. Lischer challenges the use of illustrations on the basis that they are not formative in helping people become disciples.
45. In African settings, worship should be interesting or "exciting." See J. W. K. Mugambi and Laurenti Magesa, eds., *The Church in African Christianity: Innovative Essays in Ecclesiology* (Nairobi, Kenya: Initiatives Publishers, 1990), p. 46. "Exciting" worship is specifically experienced in African independent churches.
46. Sweazey, *Preaching the Good News*, pp. 193–95.
47. Buttrick, *Homiletic*, p. 133.
48. Spain, *Getting Ready to Preach*, pp. 84–87.
49. English, *Evangelical Theology of Preaching*, p. 134.
50. Allen, *Interpreting the Gospels*, p. 165. For similar views, see Buttrick, *Homiletic*, p. 83, 90–91; Lewis, *Persuasive Preaching*, p. 181; and Jordan, *You Can Preach*, p. 115.
51. Sherry, ed., *The Riverside Preachers*, p. 103. This is the way Ernest Campbell, one of the Riverside Preachers, saw it. The Riverside Church in New York was blessed to have preachers of high repute in its pulpit.
52. Grace Mutandwa, "MDC Lays on the Charm in ZANU-PF for Chitungwiza," *The Financial Gazette*, 11–17 November 1999, p. 6.
53. McNulty, ed., *Preaching Better*, p. 4.
54. For details of this concept we refer again to Craddock, *Overhearing the Gospel*.
55. W. B. Riley, *The Preacher and His Preaching* (Wheaton, IL: Sword of the Lord Publishers, 1948), p. 143.
56. For these experiences with the African's sense of humour in (Zaire) DRC, see Almquist, *Debtor Unashamed*, p. 22.
57. Although homileticians pay attention to the use of humour in sermons to varying degrees, one would find most helpful ideas and guidelines in Bob Parrot, *God's Sense of Humour: Where? When? How?* (New York: Philosophy Library, 1984), pp. 8–171. See similar points and a variety of views in Sweazey, *Preaching the Good News*,

pp. 201–12; Buttrick, *Homiletic*, pp. 95–96, 146–47; and Jones says Jesus Christ himself was a humorous person, see Jones, *Principles and Practice of Preaching*, p. 141.
58. Lewis, *Persuasive Preaching*, p. 152.
59. Sweazey, *Preaching the Good News*, p. 43.
60. For details on listener obstacles, see Millard J. Erickson and James L. Heflin, *Old Wine, in New Wineskins: Doctrinal Preaching in a Changing World* (Grand Rapids, MI: Baker Books, 1997), pp. 76, 78, 84.

Chapter 4: Can Preaching Be Taught?

1. Don M. Wardlaw, ed., with Fred Baumer, Donald F. Chatfield, Joan Delaplane, O.P., O. C. Edwards, Jr., Edwina Hunter, and Thomas H. Troeger, *Learning Preaching: Understanding and Participating in the Process* (Lincoln, IL: The Lincoln Christian College and Seminary Press, 1989), p. 31.
2. For the theological, ecclesiological, and cultural perspectives, see Wardlaw, ed., *Learning Preaching*, pp. 7–16.
3. For more on the life-giving Church and the proclamation of the gospel, see Bénezét Bujo, *African Theology in Its Social Context*, p. 99.
4. Eugene Hillman, *Toward an African Christianity: Inculturation Applied* (Mahwah, NJ: Paulist Press, 1993), p. 43.
5. Tsuneaki Kato, "Preaching of the Gospel in the Japan Protestant Church," in Kato, ed., *Preaching as God's Mission*, p. 239.
6. Martey, *African Theology*, pp. 63–94. See also Pobee, *Skenosis: Christian Faith in an African Context*, pp. 23–41. This is a discussion of different terminologies concerning the Africanization of doing theology.
7. Don M. Wardlaw, "Toward an Incarnational Homiletical Pedagogy," p. 2. This is a paper presented at the Societas Homiletica Conference, Virginia Seminary, Washington DC, USA, March/April, 1999.
8. See Martey, *African Theology*, pp. 56–57.
9. These findings surfaced in a sermon preached by Professor Rudolf Bohren on Matthew 5:48 at the Societas Homiletica Conference held in Berlin, Germany, 1995. The sermon was printed and circulated to participants.
10. Helge Beden Nielsen, "Pastoral Care and Homiletics," in Kato, ed., *Preaching as God's Mission*, p. 180.
11. Bujo, *African Theology*, p. 69.
12. Manfred Josuttis, "Preaching with the Authority of the Sermon on the Mount," a paper presented at the Societas Homiletica, Berlin, German, June 1995, p. 3.
13. John de Gruchy, *Cry Justice: Prayers, Meditations and Readings from South Africa* (Maryknoll, NY: Orbis Books, 1986), p. 88.
14. See K. P. Kasambira, *Teaching Methods*, reprint 1995, 1997 (Harare, Zimbabwe: College Press Publishers, Ltd., 1993) p. 132.
15. Wendland, *Preaching that Grabs the Heart*, pp. 237–38.

Chapter 5: Summary

1. The 7th General Assembly of the All Africa Conference of Churches, which met in Addis Abba in 1997, chose "Troubled But Not Destroyed" as its theme. See *Tam tam* 2 (1996): 2. This is a magazine published by the All Africa Conferences of Churches (AACC) in Nairobi, Kenya.

Bibliography

Books

Abbott, Jeri, Joy Lowe, and Allen Mundeta, comps. *God at Work in Gazaland: A History of the United Church of Christ in Zimbabwe 1983–1993*. (publisher???).

Achtemeier, Elizabeth. *Creative Preaching: Finding the Words*. Edited by William D. Thompson. Nashville: Abingdon Press, 1980.

Achtemeier, Elizabeth. *Preaching as Theology and Art*. Nashville: Abingdon Press, 1984.

Allen, Ronald J. *Interpreting the Gospel: An Introduction to Preaching*. St. Louis, MO: Chalice Press, 1998.

Almquist, L. Arden. *Debtor Unashamed: The Road to Mission Is a Two Way Street*. Chicago: Covenant Publications, 1993.

Amanze, James N. *African Christianity in Botswana*. Gweru: Mambo Press, 1988.

Anderson, Allen. *Moya: The Holy Spirit in an African Context*. Pretoria: University of South Africa, 1991.

Anderson, Ray S., ed. *Theological Foundations for Ministry: Selected Readings for a Theology of the Church in Ministry*. Grand Rapids, MI: William B. Eerdmans, 1979.

Aschwanden, Herbert. *Karanga Mythology: An Analysis of the Consciousness of the Karanga in Zimbabwe*. Gweru: Mambo Press, 1987.

Barret, David B., ed. *African Initiatives in Religion*. Nairobi: East African Publishing House, 1971.

Barth, Karl. *Homiletics*. Translated by Geoffrey W. Bromiley and Donald E. Daniels. Foreword by David G. Buttrick. Louisville, KY: Westminister John Knox Press, 1966.

Baumann, Daniel J. *An Introduction to Contemporary Preaching*. Grand Rapids, M: Baker Book House, 1988.

Bausch, William J. *Storytelling, Imagination and Faith*. Mystic, CT: Twenty-Third Publications, 1986.

Bebey, Francis. *African Music: A People's Art*. Translated by Josephine Bennett. Westport, NY: Lawrence Hill & Co., 1975.

Bodey, Allen Richard, ed. *Inside the Sermon: Thirteen Preachers Discuss Their Methods of Preparing Messages*. Grand Rapids, MI: Baker Book House, 1990.

Bonhoeffer, Dietrich. *Worldly Preaching: Lectures on Homiletics*. Edited and compiled by Clyde E. Fant. New York: Crossroad Publishing Co., 1991.

Bonhoeffer, Dietrich. *Christology*. Introduction by Edwin H. Robertson. Translated by John Bowden. London: Collins, 1966.

Bourdillon, Michael. *The Shona Peoples: An Ethnography of the Contemporary Shona with Special Reference to Their Religion*. Rev. ed. Gweru: Mambo Press, 1998.

Bourdillon, Michael. *Religion and Society: A Text for Africa*. Gweru: Mambo Press, 1990.

Brooks, Phillips. *Lectures on Preaching*. Grand Rapids, MI: Zondervan, n.d.

Browne, R. E. C. *The Ministry of the Word*. London: SCM Press, 1976.

Brueggemann, Walter. *Cadences of Home: Preaching Among Exiles*. Louisville, KY: Westminister John Knox Press, 1997.

Bujo, Bénezét. *African Theology in Its Social Context*. Translated by John O'Donohue. Maryknoll, NY: Orbis Books, 1992.

Buttrick, David. *Homiletic, Moves and Structures*. Philadelphia: Fortress Press, 1987.

Calkins, Raymond. *The Eloquence of Christian Experience*. New York: McMillan Co., 1927.

Chipenda, Jose B., Andre Karamaga, J. N. K. Mugambi, and C. K. Omari, eds. *The Church of Africa: Towards a Theology of Reconstruction*. Nairobi: All Africa Conference of Churches, 1991.

Cleland, James T. *Preaching To Be Understood*. Nashville: Abingdon Press, 1965.

Confessions of St. Augustine. Translated and introduction by John K. Ryan. Book I, chap. 1. New York: Image Books, Doubleday, 1960.

Craddock, Fred B. *Preaching*. Nashville: Abingdon Press, 1985.

Craddock, Fred B. *Overhearing the Gospel*. Nashville: Abingdon Press, 1978.

Craddock, Fred B. *As One Without Authority*. Nashville: Abingdon Press, 1979.

Crum, Milton, Jr. *Manual on Preaching: A New Process of Sermon Development*. Valley Forge, PA: Judson Press, 1977.

Daneel, Inus M. *Quest for Belonging: Introduction to a Study of African Independent Churches*. Gweru: Mambo Press, 1987.

de Gruchy, John. *Cry Justice: Prayers, Meditations and Readings from South Africa*. Maryknoll, NY: Orbis Books, 1986.

Duke, Robert W. *The Sermon as God's Word: Theologies for Preaching*. Edited by William D. Thompson. Nashville: Abingdon Press, 1980.

Edwards, O. C., Jr. *Elements of Homiletic: A Method for Preparing to Preach*. Collegeville, MN: Pueblo Publishing Co., 1982.

Éla, Jean-Marc. *My Faith as an African*. Translated by John Pairman and Susan Perry. Maryknoll, NY: Orbis Books, 1988.

Ellingsen, Mark. *The Integrity of Biblical Narrative: Story in Theology and Proclamation*. Minneapolis: Fortress Press, 1990.

Forbes, James A. *Holy Spirit and Preaching*. Nashville: Abingdon Press, 1989.

Fortress, David F. *The Modern Theologians: An Introduction to Christian Theology in the Twentieth Century*. 2nd ed. Malden, MA: Blackwell Publishers, 1997.

Forde, Daryll, ed. *African Worlds: Studies in the Cosmological Ideas and Social Values of African Peoples*. London: Oxford University Press, 1991.

Gelfand, Michael. *Ukama: Reflections on Shona and Western Cultures in Zimbabwe*. Gweru, Zimbabwe: Mambo Press, 1981.

Garrison, Webb B. *The Preacher and His Audience*. New York: Fleming H. Revell Co., n.d.

Hamutyinei, Mordikai A., and Albert B. Plangger. *Tsumo-Shumo: Shona Proverbial Lore and Wisdom*. Gweru, Zimbabwe: Mambo Press, 1974.

Hannan, M. S. J. *Standard Shona Dictionary*. Harare, Zimbabwe: College Press, 1984.

Harris, James H. *Preaching Liberation*. Minneapolis: Augsburg Fortress Press, 1995.

Hickman, Hoyt L. *A Primer for Church Worship*. Nashville: Abingdon Press, 1984.

Hillman, Eugene. *Toward an African Christianity: Inculturation Applied*. Mahwah NJ: Paulist Press, 1993.

Halbert, John C. *Preaching Old Testament Proclamation and Narrative in the Hebrew Bible*. Nashville: Abingdon Press, 1991.

Holland, De Witte. *The Preaching Tradition: A Brief History*. Edited by William D. Thompson. Nashville: Abingdon Press, 1980.

Holmes, Urban T. III. *Ministry and Imagination*. New York: Seabury Press, 1976.

Horden, William E. *Speaking of God: The Nature and Purpose of Theological Language*. New York: MacMillan, 1964.

Howe, Reuel L. *Partners in Preaching: Clergy and Laity in Dialogue*. New York: Seabury Press, 1967.

Hoyt, Arthur S. *Vital Elements of Preaching*. New York: McMillan, 1923.

Hughes Robert G., and Robert Kysar. *Preaching Doctrine for the Twenty-First Century*. Minneapolis: Fortress Press, 1977.

Jabusch, Willard F. *The Person in the Pulpit*. Edited by William D. Thompson. Nashville: Abingdon Press, 1980.

Jackson, Edgar N. *A Psychology for Preaching*. Preface by Harry Emerson Fosdick. New York: Great Neck Channel Press, 1961.

Jones, Illion T. *Principles and Practice of Preaching: A Comprehensive Study of the Art of Sermon Construction*. Nashville: Abingdon Press, 1984.

Karamaga, Andre, comp. *Problems and Promises of Africa: Towards and Beyond the Year* 2000. All Africa Conference of Churches, 1993.

Kasambira, P. K. *Teaching Methods*. Harare, Zimbabwe: College Press, 1993. Reprint eds. 1995, 1997. Harare, Zimbabwe: College Press Publishers, 1997.

Kato, Tsuneaki, ed. "Preaching as God's Mission." *Studia Homiletica* 2. Tokyo: Kyo Bun Kwan, 1999.

Kemp, Charles F. ed., *Pastoral Preaching*. St. Louis: Bethany Press, 1963.

Killinger, John. *Fundamentals of Preaching*. Minneapolis: Fortress Press, 1991.

Kurewa, John Wesley Zwomunondiita. *Biblical Proclamation for Africa Today*. Nashville: Abingdon Press, 1995.

Lee, Young Jung. *Korean Preaching: An Interpretation*. Nashville: Abingdon Press, 1997.

Lewis, Ralph. *Persuasive Preaching Today*. Ann Arbor, MI: Asbury Theological Seminary, 1979.

Lischer, Richard. *The Preacher King: Martin Luther King Jr. and the Word that Moved America*. New York: Oxford University Press, 1995.

Long, Thomas G. *Preaching and the Literary Forms of the Bible*. Philadelphia: Fortress Press, 1989.

Long, Thomas G. and Edward Farley, eds. *Preaching as a Theological Task: World, Gospel, Scripture*. Louisville, KY: Westminster John Knox Press, 1996.

Lucas, Stephen E. *The Art of Public Speaking*. 5th ed. New York: McGraw-Hill, 1995.

Mandela, Nelson. *Long Walk to Freedom: The Autobiography of Nelson Mandela*. Abridged and edited by Coco Cachalia and Marc Suttner. Braamfontein, Gauteng, South Africa: Nolwazi Educational Publishers, 1998.

Markquart, Edward F. *Quest for Better Preaching: Resources for Renewal in the Pulpit*. Minneapolis: Augsburg Publishing House, 1985.

Marty, Martin E. *The Word: People Participating in Preaching*. Philadelphia: Fortress Press, 1984.

Mbefo, Nnamndi Luke. *The Reshaping of African Traditions*. Enugu, Nigeria: Spiritan Publications, 1988.

Mbiti, John S. *Introduction to African Religion*. 2nd rev. ed. Oxford: Heinemann Educational Publishers, 1991.

McNulty, Frank J. *Preaching Better*. Mahwah, NY: Paulist Press, 1985.

Milimo, J. T. *Bantu Wisdom*. Lusaka: National Educational Company of Zambia, 1972.

Morris, Colin. *The Word and the Words*. Nashville: Abingdon Press, 1975.

Moyd, Olin P. *The Sacred Art: Preaching and Theology in the African-American Tradition*. Foreword by Samuel D. Proctor. Valley Forge, PA: Judson Press, 1995.

Mugambi, J. N. K., ed. *Critiques of Christianity in African Literature: With Particular Reference to the East African Context*. Nairobi, Kenya: East African Educational Publishers, 1992.

Mugambi, J. N. K., and Laurenti Magesa, eds. *The Church in African Christianity: Innovative Essays in Ecclesiology*. Nairobi, Kenya: Initiatives Publishers, 1990.

Mukonyora, Isabel, James L. Cox, and Frans J. Verstraelen, eds. *"Re-Writing" the Bible: The Real Issues: Perspectives from within Biblical and Religious Studies in Zimbabwe*. Gweru, Zimbabwe: Mambo Press, 1993.

Mutswairo, Solomon M. *Chaminuka: Prophet of Zimbabwe.* Harare: Harper Collins Publishers, 1994.

Ndiokwere, Nathaniel. *The African Church Today and Tomorrow: Inculturation in Practice.* vol. 2. Enugu, Nigeria: SNAAP Press, 1994.

Niebuhr, Richard H. *Christ and Culture.* New York: Harper and Row, 1951.

Nhiwatiwa, Eben Kanukayi. *Humble Beginnings: A Brief History of the United Methodist Church, Zimbabwe Area, Gleanings from the Heritage of the United Methodist Church in Zimbabwe: Celebrating the Centennial.* Zimbabwe Annual Conference, 1997.

Niles, T. D. *Preaching the Gospel of the Resurrection.* Philadelphia: The Westminster Press, 1954.

Nyamiti, Charles. *Christ as Our Ancestor: Christology from an African Christian Perspective.* Gweru: Mambo Press, 1984.

Official Journal of the East Central Africa Mission Conference of the Methodist Episcopal Church, 1913.

Official Journal of the East Central Africa Mission Conference of the Methodist Episcopal Church, 1922.

Official Journal of the Rhodesia Annual Conference of the Methodist Church, 1956.

Official Journal of the Rhodesia Annual Conference of the Methodist Church,1964.

O'Day, Gail; and Thomas G. Long, eds. *Listening to the Word: Studies in Honor of Fred B. Craddock.* Nashville: Abingdon Press, 1993.

Oduyoye, Mercy Amba. *Daughters of Anowa: African Women and Patriarchy.* Maryknoll, NY: Orbis Books, 1995.

Onwubiko, Oliver A. *African Thought, Religion and Culture.* Enugu, Nigeria: SNAAP Press, 1991.

Oxman, Bromley G. *Preaching in a Revolutionary Age.* Nashville: Abingdon/Cokesbury Press, 1944.

Parrott, Bob W. *God's Sense of Humor: Where? When? How?* New York: Philosophical Library, 1984.

Pobee, J. S. *Skenosis: Christian Faith in an African Context.* Gweru: Mambo Press, 1992.

Pongweni, Alec J. C. *Figurative Language in Shona Discourse: Imagination.* Gweru, Zimbabwe: Mambo Press, 1989.

Proctor, Samuel D. *The Certain Sound of the Trumpet: Crafting a Sermon of Authority.* Valley Forge, PA: Judson Press, 1994.

Read, David H. C. *Preaching about the Needs of Real People.* Philadelphia: The Westminster Press, 1988.

Rice, Charles L. *The Embodied Word: Preaching as Art and Liturgy.* Minneapolis: Fortress Press, 1991.

Riley, W. B. *The Preacher and His Preaching.* Wheaton, IL: Sword of the Lord Publishers, 1948.

Ross, Kenneth R., ed. *Gospel Ferment in Malawi: Theological Essays*. Gweru: Mambo Press, 1995.

Schapera, I. and John L. Comaroff. *The Tswana*. Rev. ed. London: Kegan Paul International in Association with International African Institute, 1991.

Schreiter, Robert J. *Constructing Local Theologies*. Maryknoll, NY: Orbis Books, 1985.

Smith, Roy L. *Preach the Word*. Nashville: Abingdon/Cokesbury Press, 1957.

Smith, Christine M. *Preaching as Weeping, Confession, and Resistance: Radical Responses to Radical Evil*. Louisville, KY: Westminster John Knox Press, 1992.

Proctor-Smith, Marjorie. *In Her Own Rite: Constructing Feminist Liturgical Tradition*. Nashville: Abingdon Press, 1990.

Söderström, Hugo. *God Gave Growth: The History of the Lutheran Church in Zimbabwe*, 1903–1980. Gweru, Zimbabwe: Mambo Press, 1984.

Song, Choan-Seng. *Third-Eye Theology: Theology in Formation in Asian Settings*. Maryknoll, NY: Orbis Books, 1979.

Steimle, Edmund, Charles L. Rice, and Morris J. Niedenthal. *Preaching the Story*. Philadelphia: Fortress Press, 1980.

Stevenson, Dwight E. and Charles F. Diehl. *Preaching People from the Pulpit: A Guide to Effective Sermon Delivery*. New York: Harper and Row, 1958.

Stott, John R. W. *Between Two Worlds: The Art of Preaching in the Twentieth Century*. Grand Rapids, MI: William B. Eerdmans, 1982.

Swank, George W. *Dialogic Style in Preaching: More Effective Preaching Series*. Valley Forge, PA: Judson Press, 1981.

Sweazey, George E. *Preaching the Good News*. Englewood Cliffs, NJ: Prentice-Hall, Inc., 1976.

Taylor, Gardner C. *How Shall They Preach*. Elgin, IL: Progressive Baptist Publishing House, 1977.

Thangaraj, Thomas M. *Preaching as Communication*. Accra, Ghana: A Sempa Publishers, 1989.

The African Synod: Documents Reflections, Perspectives. Compiled and edited by Africa Faith and Justice Network under the direction of Maura Browne, S.N.D. Maryknoll, NY: Orbis Books, 1996.

Thielicke, Helmut. *The Trouble with the Church: A Call for Renewal*. Translated and edited by John Doberstein. New York: Harper and Row, 1965.

Thielicke, Helmut. *Encounter with Spurgeon*. Translated by John W. Doberstein. Grand Rapids, MI: Baker Book House, 1975.

Thorpe, S. A. *African Traditional Religions: An Introduction*. University of South Africa, Koedoesport: Sigma Press, 1991.

Turner, H. W. *African Independent Church: The Life and Faith of the Church of the Lord (Aladura)*. vol. 2. Oxford: Clarendon Press, 1967.

Ward, Richard F. *Speaking from the Heart: Preaching with Passion*. Nashville: Abingdon Press, 1992.

Wardlaw, Don M. ed. *Learning Preaching: Understanding and Participating in the Process*. Lincoln, IL: The Lincoln Christian College and Seminary Press, 1989.

Wendland, Ernst R. *Preaching that Grabs the Heart: A Rhetorical Stylistic Study of the Chichewa Revival Sermons of Shadrack Wame*. Foreword by Kenneth R. Ross. Blantyre, Malawi: Christian Literature Association in Malawi, 2000.

Wietzke, Walter R. *The Primacy of the Spoken Word: Redemptive Proclamation in a Complex World*. Minneapolis: Augsburg Publishing House, 1988.

Wilson, Paul Scott. *Imagination of the Heart: New Understanding in Preaching*. Nashville: Abingdon Press, 1988.

Journals and Magazines

Culver, Maurice E. "A Witness to African Religion." *Africa Christian Advocate* (July–September 1964): 2–3.

Farmer, Albert David. "Pulpit Laureate and Presidential Favorite: An Interview with Gardner Taylor." *Pulpit Digest* 77, no. 541 (September/October 1996): 97–101.

Garrett, Graeme. "Preaching in Today's World." *Pulpit Digest* 80, no. 2 (March/April 1999): 96.

"Have you ever heard of Chimanimani Musical Group?" *Parade* (November 1999).

Kurewa, John Wesley. "Can Anything Good Come Out of Africa?" *Africa Christian Advocate* (April–June 1964): 10–11.

Mafico, Temba J. "Tradition, Faith, and the Africa University." *Quarterly Review* 9, no. 2 (Summer 1998): 35–51.

Magesa, Laurenti. "Authentic African Christianity." *African Ecclesial Review* 37 (August 1995): 209–20.

McHenry, Francis, O.S.B. "The Essence of Inculturation of Christianity in Africa." *African Ecclesial Review* 37 (August 1995): 228–37.

Moila, M. P. "The Effect of Belief in the Living Dead on the Church Mission in South Africa." *Africa Theological Journal* 18 (1989): 140–49.

Mosha, Raymond S. "The Trinity in the African Context." *Africa Theological Journal* 9 (1980): 40–52.

Moyo, Mavingire Ambrose. "The Quest for African Christian Theology and the Problem of the Relationship Between Faith and Culture: The Hermeneutical Perspective." *Africa Theological Journal* 11 (1983): 95–108.

Obeng, E. A. "Inroads of African Religion into Christianity: The Case of the Spiritual Churches." *Africa Theological Journal* 16 (1987): 43–50.

Thomas, David A. "The Pulpit and Freedom of Speech," *Pulpit Digest* 77, no. 58 (March/April 1996): 81–88.

Wimberly, Edward P. "The Black Christian Experience and the Holy Spirit." *Quarterly Review* 8, no. 2 (Summer 1998): 19–35.

"Use Your Imagination with Your Salads." *Sunday Mail Magazine* (29 March 1998): 13.

Newspapers

"Five Members of Local Church Hauled in Front of Magistrate." *The Herald*, 12 January 2000, p. 5.

"The Church Must Speak Out!" *Zimbabwe Independent*, 14 April 2000, p. 6.

The Daily News, 14 April 2000, p. 8.

"N'angas 'recover' Owls Snakes, Organ from Farm Workers' Houses." *The Herald*, 6 November 1999, p. 1.

Ncube, Ivy. "Aids Threatens to Wipe Out Settlement." *The Herald*, 6 November 1999, p. 1.

Schmid, S. "Let's All Face Economic Problems as Challenges." *The Herald*, 8 November 1999, p. 6.

Theses and Papers

Debus, Gerhard, with Rudolf Bohren, Ulrich Brates, Herald Grun-Rath, and Georg Vischer. "Theses Concerning Sermon Analysis." Translated by Birgit Taylor. Paper presented at the Societas Homiletica Conference, Kyoto, Japan, 5 June 1997.

Gray, Jarret C., Jr. "Soteriological Themes In African-American Methodist Preaching, 1876–1914." PhD dissertation, Drew University, 1993.

Josuttis, Manfred. "Preaching with the Authority of the Sermon on the Mount." Paper presented at the Societas Homiletica Conference, Berlin, Germany, 28 June 1995.

Wardlaw, Don M. "Toward an Incarnational Homiletical Pedagogy." Paper presented at the Societas Homiletica Conference, Virginia Seminary, Washington, DC, USA, 3 March 1999.